An outline of Customs Policy of the Democratic Republic of Congo 2003-2010

Jean-Paul ESAMBA BOKEL'IPOKA

An outline of Customs Policy of the Democratic Republic of Congo 2003-2010

Foreword by Déo Rugwiza Magera

L'Harmattan
Cameroun

5-7, rue de l'Ecole-Polytechnique, 75005 Paris

http://www.editions-harmattan.fr

ISBN : 978-2-343-17710-6
EAN : 9782343177106

FOREWORD

On January 1st, 1995, the World Trade Organization (WTO) was created in order to realise the unsuccessful objective pursued by the States, to create the International Trade Organization (ITO) in 1948, in the wake of the economic disaster caused by the First and Second World Wars.Thus created, the WTO multilateral trading system will advocate the liberalisation of international trade for social welfare.

As for customs being at the border, it must facilitate international trade by simplifying its customs clearance procedures. In this way, towards the end of the 20th century, several states adopted the policy of reforming and modernising their customs administrations with the support of various partners, including the International Monetary Fund (IMF), the World Customs Organization (WCO), The World Bank (WB), etc.

The reform and modernisation programme also included strengthening the capacities of customs staff. Thus, on 11th May 2005, a first consultative meeting between the WCO Secretariat and universities and research institutes was held at the WCO headquarters in Brussels, Belgium. The Partnership in Customs Academic Research and Development (PICARD) programme was initiated with the aim to be indispensable to the professional development, for all customs practitioners, to become good customs decision makers by knowledge-based research, and successful by partnering with academia and other relevant stakeholders.

This allowed Mr Jean-Paul Esamba Bokel'Ipoka, author of this book entitled ***An outline of customs policy of the Democratic Republic of Congo (from 2003 to 2010)***, which I have the honor to preface as Director General of Customs and Excise of DRC, to further his Master degree in Customs Policy and Customs Administration and International trade at the University of Munster in Germany.

In connection with this programme of customs reform and modernisation, the Directorate General of Customs and Excise at the time Customs and Excise Office, designed its programme of reform and modernisation in 2003. It comprises three main areas: facilitating and simplifying customs procedures, optimising the mechanism of combating fraud, reorganising services and measures programmes.

Admittedly, this book is written in English, the first in the DRC customs administration history; he is the appropriate person to share his experience in Shakespeare's language in the field of customs policy, after his training in Germany and his professional experience at the Regional Intelligence Liaison Office for Central Africa and the Great Lakes, where he represents the DRC as Technical Attaché and an intelligence analyst.

His work, which appears to be an added value within the Congolese customs, presents pertinent theoretical and practical aspects. In the theoretical part, the author examines the question of customs policy and its basic notions. Thus, in the practical part, he uses the 2003 customs reform and modernisation programme to help readers grasp the concept of customs policy concretely; he also gives a brief evaluation of the programme of customs reform.

Déo Rugwiza Magera

Director General

DEDICATION

To you,

My wife Antoinette Pauline Loota Nkisi,

My sons Robert Esamba Bas'Ikonga and Fernand Ivovu Esamba,

My daughters Sephora Beese Bas'Esamba, Ketshia Bekembo Esamba and Veronique Petra Bopenda B'Esamba,

My parents late father Faustin Esamba Ndjokonda and my mother Cécile Beese Ngonga,

The DRC Customs experts who designed the 2003 customs reform and modernisation programme.

ACKNOWLEDGMENTS

To start with, I would like to pay tribute to the Cameroon government and its customs administration for their warm hospitality without which this book would not be written during my stay in Cameroon.

My special gratitude is expressed to H.E Madam Minette Libom Likeng, current Minister of Post and TeleCommunication and former Customs Director General, Mr Edwin Fongod Nuvada, Cameroon customs Director General, Ndo Gervais, Tafili Ebenezer, Samson Bilagna, Felicien Mballa, Grégoire Biloa, Samuel Kouam, Thierry Zogo, Djeuwo Marcellin, Madam Ilunga, Essoh Ewane and their staff, Bertrand Toukap, Clémentine Kanse, Anne Teclaire and others.

At the end of this work, I wish to express my gratitude and appreciation to Prof. Wieslaw "Wes" Czyzowicz for his unfailing patience and help during this book redaction.

I express my deep thanks to the DRC customs and Excise Director General, Mr. Deo Rugwiza Magera for his support of many kinds; Deputy Director Generals Big Nzuka Mapengo and Nkongolo Kabila for their moral support.

Grateful acknowledgment is due to the former President Managing Directors Juvenal Lufuma Makanda and Albert Kasongo Mukonzo, Directors Anicet Belito Belie and late Sylvain Balonga be Bokfa who welcomed us to the DRC customs and Excise community.

Grateful acknowledgement is also due to Directors Kiesse-A-Ngunda, Nianda Malanda, Kuburanwa Chirimwami, Mupenda Kabwana, Mubibya Silutala, Ernest Kassondimbwa, yoram Eciba, Patrice Mbuaki, Ngbanda Eponge, Epondo Eso, Magera Bakure, late Selemani SAM, President of syndicate Désiré Itegwa, Didier Nendaka, Mogugo and Deputy Director Mukuna Katumba for their moral support.

I also acknowledge my trainers from different Universities, the World Customs Organization and others who did their best for my English education namely: Ordinary Prof. Majambo Kalonda, Prof. Katsuva Ngoloma, Prof. Mubenga, Prof. Achim Rogmann, Prof. Michael Wolfgang, Prof. Harisson, Prof. Altemoller, Prof. Chiwengo, Prof. Mutoke, Prof. N'landu, CT. Kamwema Sha Mwana, CT Lombela Poyo, late Kombe Kabedi Thierry Pirreau, Pierre Devaucher, Sebastien Costa and others.

I am indebted to Dr. Judith Hoffmann, Deputy Director Fidel Ramazani Radjabu, Jacques N'lemo and my colleagues from SADC for their moral support during my training attendance in Germany.

It is impossible to provide a complete list of people who supported me morally or materially and others to whom I am obliged, for valuable information and all kinds of assistance. In some cases, I acknowledge, Bishop Gérard Mulumba, Father Lambert Moseka, late Father Eric, Aubert Buhake, late Donatien Mujinga, Madam Ana Hinojosa, Motoyuki Okura, Souleymane Sangare, Elsie Lemami, Bernard Zbinden, Edmond Galle, Michelle Medina, Norbert Steilen, Marc Bruneau, Richard Soki, Adam Vas, Petra Heininger, Dr Karim Farat, André Monga, Jean Fidel Yakala, Gustave Intemo, Phelly

Kitenge, Aaron Cianyi, Monique Mpumpu, Boale Jeff and Désiré Mawe for their moral support.

I owe special gratitude to my colleagues from the Rilo Global Network: Pierre Bertrand, Loic Gunn, Agnieszka Butrym Bielatko, Iwona Sawicka, François Remue, Daniela Dettmann, Katarzyna Banaszek, Gonzalo, Duncan Potter, Nizar, Faisal, Magdalena Rybaczyk, Sylvia Paczuska, Anette Bonde,Gaspard Cillufoli, Laurent Pinot, Abdoul Jeng, Ibrahim Agassalat, Samba Thiam,Santouma, Bede, (…), RILO Central Africa staff, namely: Etienne Sama 2, Altesse Samake, Raissa Nkolo, Véro Manimben, Ngo Ngijol Diane, Dieudonné Tschokwe, Cendrine Mbelle, Eric Engol and Mbeng Elise..

Special thanks are extended to the staff of the DRC Embassy in Cameroon, namely H.E Emile Okoto, Chargé d'Affaires, Jonathan Tanga, Celestin Musambali, James Sekele and Madam Jacquie for their moral support.

Special thanks are also extended to the University of Munster and its staff and to the German Government for all their assistance during my training in Germany.

Special gratitude is expressed to my uncles Emile Baondje, Médard Belemo, late Anaclet Belanga, my late brother Emery Mbalosanga, my brother Abbé Robert Esamba, my cousin Eric Baondje, my aunt Odette Mpembe and all my sisters, brothers and relatives.

May my Colleagues, friends and relatives whose names are not quoted in this book, find the expression of my gratitude for any kind of support for this book publication.

ABBREVIATIONS

ABAKO: Alliance des Bakongo (Alliance of Bakongo)

ACP: African Caribbean and Pacific Group of States

AD: from Latin, Anno Domini. Used in the Christian calendar to show a particular number of years since the year when Christ was believed to have been born.

ADF NALU/ADF-NALU: Allied Democratic Forces

AEO: Agreed Economic Operator

AFDL: Alliance des Forces Démocratiques pour la Libération du Congo (Democratic Alliance Forces for the liberation of Congo)

AGOA: African Growth and Opportunity Act

AL Shebab/Al-Shabab: young fighters movement, it is a Somalian Islamist terrorist group.

AL-QUAIDA : a loosely-knit militant Islamic organization led and funded by Osama bin Laden

API : Advanced Passanger Information

AQMI : Al-Qaeda in the Islamic Maghreb. It is an Islamist militant organization (of al-Qaeda)

ASYCUDA - Automated System for Customs Data

ATA: Admission temporaire, Temporary Admission

BIVAC: Bureau Inspection Valuation Assessment Control

BW: Biological Weapon

CA: Central Africa

CCC: Customs Co-operation Council

CEN: Customs Enforcement Network

CENcomm: Customs Enforcement Network for Communication

CKD: Complete Knocked Down

COMESA: Common Market for Eastern and Southern Africa

CONFIAD: Confédération Internationale des Agents en Douane (International Federation of Customs Brokers and Customs Representatives)

COP: Conference of Parties

COPIC: COPIC Marker is high quality marker for industrial design, architecture design, fashion design, graphics, illustrations, craft, model design.

CW: Chemical Weapon

DDCOM: Déclaration Douanière du Comesa (Comesa cutoms declaration)

DGDA : Direction Générale des Douanes et Accises (Directorate General of Customs and Excise)

DRC: Democratic Republic of Congo

EAC: Eastern African Community

EC: Enforcement Committee

ECCAS: Economic Community of Central African States

ECGLC: Economic Community of the Great Lakes Countries

EGL: Embedded-System Graphics Library

ENF: Ecole Nationale des Finances (National School of Finances)

EPA: Economic Partnership Agreement

EU: European Union

FCTC: Framework Convention on Tobacco Protocol

FMCG: Fast-Moving Consumer Goods

FOS: Framework of Standard

FTA: Free Trade Agreement

FTA: Free Trade Area

FTA: Free Trade Association

GATS: General Agreement in Trade of Services

GATT: General Agreement on Tariff and Trade

GS: Global Shield

GSP: Generalised System of Preferences

H.E: His Excellency

H.S: Harmonised System

H5N1: A virus subtype that occurs mainly in birds, is highly contagious among birds, and can be deadly to them

HQ: Headquaters

ICA: Impôt sur le Chiffre d'Affaires (Tax on turnover)

ICC: International Chamber of Commerce

ICT: Information and Communication Technology

IEDS: Improvised Explosive Devices

IMF: International Monetary Fund

INTERPOL: International Criminal Police Organization

IPM: Interface Public Member

IPR: Intellectual Property Rights

ISIL: Islamic State of Iraq and the Levant

ITO: International Trade Organization

IVECO: Industrial Vehicles Corporation

Kwh: Kilowatt-hours

MAA: Mutual Administrative Assistance

MKD: Medium Knocked Down

MNC: Mouvement National Congolais (Congolese National Movement)

MOU: Memorandum of Understanding

NATO: North Atlantic Treaty Organization

nCEN: National Customs Enforcement Network

NGO: Non-Governmental Organization

Non-LDCs: Non-Least Developed Countries

NPT: Non Proliferation Treaty

NW: Nuclear Weapon

OCC: Office Congolais de contrôle (Congolese Control Office)

OFIDA: Office des Douanes et Accises (Office of Customs and Excises)

PILCAM: société camerounaise de fabrication de piles électriques (Cameroonian company for the manufacture of electric batteries)

PNR : Passenger Name Recorder

RDTCS : Radio Diagnostic Trouble Codes

RILO-CA: Regional Intelligence Liaison Office for Central Africa

RILOS: Regional Intelligence Liaison Offices

RKC: Revised Kyoto Convention

ROCBS: Regional Office for Capacity Buildings

SADC: Southern African Development Community

SALW: Small Arms and Light Weapons

STCE: Strategic Trade Control Enforcement

TIR: Transit international routier, International Road Transit

TRIPS: Trade-Related Aspects of Intellectual Property Rights

UN: United Nations

UNALOR: Union Allumettiere Equatoriale(Equatorial Match making Union)

UNCTAD: United Nations Conference on Trade and Development

UNESCO: United Nations Organisation for Education, Science and Culture

UNIDO: United Nations Industrial Development Organisation

UNODC: United Nations Office on Drugs and Crime

USA: United States of America

UTEXAFRICA: Usine Textile d'Afrique(African Textile Factory)

WA: West Africa

WCO: World Customs Organization

WHO: World Health Organization

WIPO: World Intellectual Property Organization

WMD: Weapon of Mass Destruction

WTO: World Trade Organization

OUTLINE

FOREWORD 5

DEDICATION 7

ACKNOWLEDGMENTS 9

ABBREVIATIONS 13

INTRODUCTION 21

CHAPTER 1 AN OVERVIEW OF THE DEMOCRATIC REPUBLIC OF CONGO AND ITS CUSTOMS ADMINISTRATION 25

CHAPTER 2 THE BASICS OF CUSTOMS POLICY 39

CHAPTER 3 THE SECURITY MISSION OF CUSTOMS 65

CHAPTER 4 THE CUSTOMS POLICY OF THE DEMOCRATIC REPUBLIC OF CONGO FROM 2003 TO 2010 79

CHAPTER 5 THE FUTURE OF CUSTOMS POLICY OF THE DRC 127

CONCLUSION 139

BIBLIOGRAPHY 141

TABLE OF CONTENTS 149

INTRODUCTION

The history of the Democratic Republic of Congo (DRC) Customs started a long time ago. From its beginning up to now, this administration has undergone some changes such as in 1919(creation of customs office of Congo Belge),1979(creation of OFIDA), 2003(implementation of reform and modernisation programme), 2009(creation of DGDA), 2010(another reform and modernisation programme), just to name a few. Among these innovations, one of them has got a particular positive impact on the DRC customs and deserves attention to date. This is the Programme of customs Reform and Modernisation 2003.

Whatever his mental capacity, any human being seeks to do something in life: that is what the African culture considers as a "journey motif". That means, when an African makes a trip or a journey, there is a goal, an aim or a purpose that he pursues. It is proper to say that, once born, the human being needs to make his history, what Americans call, "American dream". This explains, la raison d'être of this book: *An outline of customs policy of the Democratic Republic of Congo (from 2003-2010)*.

We were born, we have made the most part of our life in customs and we need to share our experience as a *souvenir* or a legacy to the new generation. We deem, the appropriate way to do that, is to write this book for the simple reason that, "words fly away, writings remain".

Some readers may ask themselves, why customs policy rather than focusing on other customs aspects like valuation, legislation, etc.; and why the period of 2003 to 2010?

The answers to this question are the following:

Firstly, when we joined customs in 1998 we found some documents related to the DRC customs such as the Décret du 29Janvier 1949 (Decree of January 1949), Droit douanier zairois 1996 (Zairian Customs Law) published by Mr. Alexis Ntambwe Mwamba, Tarifs des Droits et Taxes à l'importation et à l'exportation (1997); but the implementation of customs reform and modernisation in 2003 was specific and drew our attention in that, it brought a new landscape in the DRC customs management. In other words, the implementation of customs reform and modernisation in 2003 brought a new vision. It seems to be considered like the beginning of a new era, a revolution in the DRC customs management.

Secondly, for those who did not pay attention to the programme and do not know much about it or customs policy, this book appears like an opportunity to present how far the 2003 customs reform and modernisation programme embodies the customs policy of the DRC during the era we are talking about; and they have to pay attention to any forth coming reform and modernisation programme in the DRC customs.

Finally, there is not much literature about the DRC customs. This book seems to be an added value one. Furthermore, customs field is huge; it would not be pertinent to deal with all its aspects. Limiting the study on the customs policy within a specific period would be more effective.

This book is outlined as follows:

The first chapter talks about the DRC and its customs administration. It displays the country historically, geographically, economically, culturally and linguistically, to help the reader get some knowledge about the country we are dealing with. A brief account of customs and that of Customs and Excise Directorate General of the DRC from the beginning to date are also presented. Developing those aspects would be important in order to better perceive the DRC customs policy.

The second chapter attempts to define what customs policy is, its objects, elements, sources, roles or functions, instruments, creators and measures. It gives the reader the possibility to learn the lexic of customs policy. That is, different words which are used in trade in goods.

The third chapter develops the importance of security in any domain especially in customs. It shows how security is very important for customs to perform its role; levying customs duties, combating fraud, protecting local economy, environment, etc. Emphasis is also placed on the WCO initiatives taken on this issue especially its security programme.

The fourth chapter constitutes the cornerstone of the book; it stresses on the DRC customs policy from 2003 to 2010. Emphasis is especially put on the 2003 programme of customs reform and modernisation, the book considers to be the customs policy of the DRC from 2003 to 2010. The chapter summarises that 2003 programme and shows its key elements. Other aspects related to the customs reform and modernization policy such as cooperation with regional and international organizations are taken into account as well.

It places also stress on the Bali package and underlines the importance of trade facilitation convention for today and the future of customs and business all of the world. The fifth chapter, finally, foresees what should be the future of the DRC customs policy. It displays determinants and future missions of the customs policy of the DRC, difficulties for developing countries among which the

DRC to implement determinants, missions, remedies and post period after the implementation of any customs policy in the Democratic Republic of Congo.

CHAPTER 1

AN OVERVIEW OF THE DEMOCRATIC REPUBLIC OF CONGO AND ITS CUSTOMS ADMINISTRATION

This chapter deals with the Democratic Republic of Congo historically, geographically, economically, culturally and linguistically. It aims at helping the reader to know more about the country concerned in its aspects, and particularly its customs administration and its customs missions.

A. BRIEF ACCOUNT OF THE DEMOCRATIC REPUBLIC OF CONGO

There is a lot to say about the DRC; but shortly, one can consider some aspects.

I. Historical aspect

The DRC history can be divided into the following periods: pre-colonial period, colonial period and post-colonial period.

1. Pre-Colonial Period

Formerly, African histories were told by means of oral tradition and via tales, proverbs, etc. Through these stories, people learnt how Africans used to live in the past. That is, their customs, cultures, etc. As the cultural heritage, the oral tradition was transmitted from generation to generation.

Concerning States, it should be noted that before the colonial period, the black continent had States that were characterised by a dense population, abundant natural wealth and flourishing arts[1].

Those States were ruled under kingdoms, empires such as the Ghana empire founded by the Soyinkés people in the 13th century, Mali empire led by Soundjiata Keita, Songhai empire ruled by Sonni Ali, Ali ber or Ali le Grand in the Western Africa[2].

In Central Africa, particularly in the Democratic Republic of Congo, empires and kingdoms which constituted different governments, existed here and there as well. Mention can be made of the Kuba kingdom founded by Chamba Bolongongo, the empire of Luba founded by Nkongolo Mwana and Kalala Ilunga in the centre of Congo[3]. In 1482, Portuguese discovered the Kongo Kingdom, on the low Congo, which was founded in the 13th century by the hunter and talisman Ntinu Wene or Nimi-a-Lukeni named Manicongo meaning the King of Congo[4].

Concerning its population, the DRC was inhabited by pygmies followed by Bantus and Nilotics.

It should be noted, however, that initially, the term Bantu means a community of languages; it gradually

---

[1] G. Mokhtar, *Histoire Générale de l'Afrique, II : l'Afrique ancienne*, Paris, Présence africaine, Edicef, Unesco 1981, p. 106.

[2] Ibrahima Baba Kaké, *Combats pour l'histoire africaine*, Présence africaine, 1985, p. 138.

[3] https:Afr.wikipedia.org/wiki/royaume-kuba. Accessed on 23 May, 2018.

[4] Ibrahima Baba Kaké, op.cit., p.139. See also Syllabus d'histoire, 5e primaire, année 2017-2018, pp. 11-23. Collège Boyokani, Kinshasa, DRCongo, see also Babudaa Malibato, *Condensé du cours complet, 6è secondaire*, Nathan, Paris 1990, pp. 38-59.

acquired an ethnographic or even anthropological connotation[5].

2. Colonial Period

Historically, Western people, especially European, arrived in the Africa continent even before the 16th century. Even if they were present since that period, Europeans conquered African States only from 1800 to 1881. Doing so, they faced some resistance from some traditional leaders such as: EL HAJ OMAR, SAMONY, RABAT.[6]. Concerning the DRC, after the Berlin Conference, held from November 1884 to February 1885, which was organised by the first German Chancellor OTTO VON BISMARCK to establish the rules that were to govern the colonisation of Africa[7], DRC became the personal property of the Belgian King LEOPOLD II. This permitted him to become very rich.

However, during the LEOPOLD II era the colonisation had a negative impact on the Congolese population living conditions. As result, this black period characterised by violence and oppression against the population accelerated the independence of the DRC which got its sovereignty on the 30th June, 1960.

3. Post Independence Period

Once independent, the DRC was ruled by Joseph KASA-VUBU as President and Patrice Emery LUMUMBA as Prime Minister.

From 1960 to 1965, DRC was in a chaotic situation. The instability in the country was an incentive for

---

[5] G. Mokhtar, op.cit., p. 456.

[6] *Ibidem*, p.106.

[7] htpps: //en.wikipedia.org/wiki/berlin-conference. Accessed on 20 May, 2018.

MOBUTU to make a coup and take power on 24th November 1965. He therefore became the second President of Congo he promised to rule for five years.[8]

After some years, he changed the Democratic Republic of Congo to Zaire with reference to the "great Nzaidi kingdom of Amboundou local people founded by Nimia Loukeni from the Eastern part and which existed in the inferior court of the Congo".[9] MOBUTU had ruled Zaire not for five years as he promised but for 32 ones.

In 1996, the rebellion led by Laurent Désiré KABILA sacked MOBUTU from power. In May 2007, Laurent Désiré KABILA became the third President of Zaire that he renamed again the Democratic Republic of Congo until now.

In January 2001, KABILA was assassinated in Kinshasa and his son Joseph KABILA replaced him.

Shortly, the DRC has undergone five republics since its independence so far.

The first Republic ruled by Joseph KASA-VUBU after the independence started from 1960 to 1965, the second Republic ruled by MOBUTU SESE SEKO KUKU NGWENDO WA ZABANGA from 1965 to 1997, the third Republic ruled by Laurent Désiré KABILA from 1997 to 2001, the fourth republic ruled by Joseph Kabila from 2001 to 2018 and to date the fifth one headed by Felix Antoine Tshisekedi Tshilombo elected president of the republic after the 30.12.2018 elections.

---

[8] Democratic Republic of the Congo: en.wiki/Democratic Republic_of_the_congo, Accessed on 28 April 2009. See also S. Jean-Paul Esamba Bokel'Ipoka, C*ounterfeiting and piracy in import and export; ''a strategy of the Democratic Republic of Congo (Master Thesis),* Muenster, University of Muenster, 2008, p. 16.

[9] Joseph Kizerbo, *Histoire de l'Afrique noire d'hier à demain*, Paris, Hatier, 1978, p.182.

II. Geographic aspect

Formerly Zaire, named by some people a subcontinent and by others the land of ancestors, the DRC is a country where by a lot of provinces are surrounded by the river Congo (Zaire). Its neighbouring countries are: Angola, Burundi, Central African Republic, Republic of Congo, Rwanda, South Sudan, Tanzania, Uganda and Zambia. Due to its population of over 75 millions and the area of 2345000 square meters, the DRC is the largest country in central Africa. Just to have a clearer image, it is large as Britain, France, Belgium, Germany, Ireland, Netherlands, Denmark, Portugal, Switzerland, Armenia, Spain, Albania and Italy put together[10]. Its capital city is Kinshasa, formerly, Leopoldville, with more than 10.000.000 inhabitants. DRC has eleven provinces which have been split into 26 ones. These new provinces are: Mongala, Bas-Uele, Haut-Uele, Ituri, Tshopo, Tshuapa, Equateur, Mai-Ndombe, Nord-Ubangi, Sud-Ubangi, Sud–Kivu, Nord-Kivu, Sankuru, Maniema, Tanganyika, Haut-Lomami, Lomami, Haut-Katanga, Lualaba, Kasai Central, Kasai Oriental, Kasai, Kwilu, Kwango, Kongo Central and Kinshasa.

III. Economic aspect

The DRC is an amazing country; each period, new mineral resources are discovered. That is why, it is recognised worldwide as a "geological scandal". Without going deeply into other aspects of economy, in terms of mineral resources, that country is very rich; the list is not

[10] Noury, Valerie, new African: the curse of coltan: DR Congo's Mineral wealth…, http://www.questiaschool.com /read/1G1-224534703/the-curse… Accessed on April 11, 2015.

exhaustive but according to Valerie NOURY[11], there are 50 ones. The DRC exports: industrial diamond, other precious or semi-precious stones, cobalt ores and concentrates, copper ores and concentrates, gold, tin ores and concentrates, zinc and alloys.[12]

IV. Cultural aspect

When we speak of culture, it is arts, dance, music; in short, people customs or identity. The DRC has more than 450 ethnic groups. It is known worldwide especially via its music. Great figures are: Kabasele Tshamala Grand Kallé, Papa Wendo, Franco Luambo Makiadi, Rochereau Tabu Ley, Lutumba Simaro, Lita Bembo, Mbuta Mashakado, Papa Wemba, Djuna Djanana, Koffi Olomide, Félix Wazekwa, Kanda Bongo, Ray Lema, Abeti Masikini, Tshala Muana, Mpongo Love, Reddy Amisi, Kabasele Yampanya Pepe Kalle, Nyoka Longo, Madilu Système, Mbilia Bel, Lokwa Kanza, King Kester Emeneya, Grand-père Bozi Boziana, Papy Tex, Bipoli, J.B. Mpiana, Ngiama Werrason, Fally Ipupa, Férré Gola, Fabregas, Adolphe Dominguez and others. The Congo is also known for its traditional works of arts which include masks and statues made of woods.

Today, there are a lot of museums with more than 45000 works of arts in Kinshasa[13] .The Congolese works of arts such as : Pende, especially the Kuba ones which have not only masks, wooden statues but also textiles

---

[11] Noury, Valerie, New African: the curse of coltan DRCongo's Mineral wealth…: //www.questiaschool.com/read/191-224534703/the-curse… Accessed on April 11, 2015

[12] United Nations conference on Trade and development, *Handbook of that world mineral trade statistica*, 1991-1996, 1997; pp. 34-40, 187-195, 304-345. See also Jean-paul Esamba Bokel Ipoka *Counterfeiting and piracy in import and export; a strategy of the democratic republic of congo* (Master Thesis), University of Muenster, 2008.

[13] B-One Radio Television watched on May 20, 2018.

made of raffia, are among the best known arts in the world.[14]

V. Linguistic aspect

The language also constitutes the vehicle of one's culture. The DRC is composed of Kongo people, Luba, Anamongo (Mongo, Ndengese, Tetela, Ntomba, Topoke, Nkundo, Ekonda, etc.), Pende, Swahili people (living in the Eastern part of the country although they have their intralinguistic and tribal differences). The list of the DRC inhabitants is not exhaustive.

Linguistically, the Democratic Republic of Congo has more than 450 dialects, four national languages namely, Lingala, Kikongo, Swahili and Tshiluba a part from the French imposed in the administration by the History, which is the official one.

Concerning these languages one can say that Lingala is spoken in the former province of Equator and its new provinces, in Kinshasa and is also the language for musicians and the army. Kikongo is spoken in the former province of Bandundu and its new provinces and in Kongo Central (Bas-Congo ex Bas-Zaire), Tshiluba is spoken in Kasai provinces and Swahili in the Eastern part of the country.

However, it should be noted that this linguistic situation may change due to the creation of new provinces. It is to the future provincial authorities to decide which language will be the main one to be spoken in their provinces.

---

[14] Kuba people are originating from the Mweka territory in the Kasai province, DRCongo.

B. DEMOCRATIC REPUBLIC OF CONGO CUSTOMS ADMINISTRATION

I. A short glance at the history of customs and its missions

It is necessary to have an overview of customs in general, before talking about the DRC customs history.

Since the domain of trade in goods seems to be defined primarily in terms of its fiscal role, one can say that Customs has been existing since humanity because people exchange, export, import and impose some duties, taxes whether internal, external or not in one way or another all the time. Since cultures differ, each geographical region got its own way of doing trade.

In Ndengese tribes[15] for example, in the ancient times, people used to do what we call in French "troc", in English "barter". That is, a kind of trade based on goods exchange. The money used on that issue was called "djelo", in French, "cauris" and in English, cowrie. "It is a small shiny shell that was used as money in the past in parts of Africa and Asia"[16]. The measure unit was "Isangi", in plural Tosangi. Each Isangi got ten djelo "cauris".It means, for example, if you want to buy a chicken which costs 5 tosangi, you have to give the seller 50 djelo (cowries) for the simple reason that 5 tosangi are multiplied by 10 which equal 50[17].

---

[15] Ndengese are people from the Dekese territory located in the North of Kasai province, Democratic Republic of Congo.

[16] Sally Wehnmeiver, *oxford advanced learner dictionary*, oxford, 2000, p.269.

[17] Bamba, the chief of Tfunga village located 5 km away from the Dekese territory headquarters, interview with Bampembe Modeste, Kinshasa, April 2015.

ASAKURA brings a strong argument to prove that Customs itself is a very ancient fiscal mechanism and perhaps one of the oldest ways of collecting money. He says that although the origins of the customs are lost, in some regions of the world its activities can be traced back to remote antiquity.

ASAKURA certifies that he is unable to prove the existence of the ancient customs service. However, he quotes valuable studies of many researchers such as the study of the Roman Customs duty[18] by R. CAGNAT, 1880, the Roman Empire, China and the Indian Sub-continent which tell that Diplomats were 78 already being exempted from customs duty in Greece, Rome, and the Indian Sub-continent at least as long as 2000 ago that the first Customs tariff was drawn up in A.D.[19] However, the problem lies on the history or origin of this kind of trade in goods known as "Customs" today. Customs, "douane" in French, "Zoll" in German, "clo" in Polish and "Dogana" in Albania, is originating from the Arabic "diouan" term itself from the Persian "diwan" (Turkish). Originally, the word meant the place where the directors of finances held their meetings. Taxes are basically the origin of customs duties[20]. Concerning the organisation of Customs as a modern service, the French customs deems that Jean Baptiste Colbert (1619-1683), Controller-General of Finance under Louis XIV, is considered to be the father of modern customs due to his economic action. It means, upon his arrival on business he focused on the economic role of

---

[18] Portorium for Romans.

[19] Asakura H., *World history of the customs and tariffs*. Brussels, World Customs Organisation, 2003, p.120.

[20] www.douane.gouv.fr Accessed on 02 April, 2015.

customs duties and the importance of customs tariff on this issue.[21]

Talking about missions, as said above, one can argue that the history of customs is connected to that of taxes and duties.

Indeed, the customs mission has evolved many years ago. Since centuries customs has been dealing with fiscal matters. In addition to this mission, the economic and social roles have been added. At the end of the 20th century, the external trade facilitation time arrived. After September 11, 2001, a new paradigm appeared. That is, "security"[22]. Customs is obliged to balance control with trade facilitation by using the risk management technique.

After being through the customs history, let us talk about the DRC customs one.

II. The DRC customs before independence

As previously said, trade in goods had been existing since humanity. Concerning Africa, in particular the DRC, a part from the barter as it was the case with the Dekese territory and elsewhere, we deem that even though the two words **customs** and **excise** were not used in the former time, may be due to the lack of written sources, trade in goods had existed even before the formation of the Republic of Zaire or Democratic Republic of Congo State as known to date. The reason is clear. African history reveals that "in the ninth century, miners from Katanga sank copper-shaped ingots in the shape of a Saint Andrew cross. Parts of all these metals were exported, another

[21] ww.musee-douanes.fr/documentation/25-histoire-de-la-douane.html.fr. Accessed on 02 April, 2018.

[22] Prof.Wieslaw Czyzowicz, Phd, Customs Policy, Module-Challenges and Futures course, Master of Customs Administration, Universisty of Muenster, Germany, May 15-16,2017, p. 21.

worked on the spot."[23] Experience has shown that some local people seem to continue with the same kind of trade in the Katanga province to date.

As argued in the part devoted to the DRC history, after the Berlin Conference in 1885, the Congo became the ownership of Leopold II, the Belgium King. It means, during the Congo Independent State, Customs existed, but its headquarter remained at Anvers in Belgium due to the fact that Congo was under the Belgian power[24].The Congolese modern customs started in the 19th century. However, the excise duties were levied in the 20th century. During this colonial period the Belgian King Leopold II imposed rights on the export of ivory, rubber and some agricultural products for his own interest and that of his country, since the Berlin conference resolutions stated the issues of trade in the Congo basin[25].

III. The DRC customs after independence (from the 15th/05/ 1979 to date)

The Congo Customs as a full administration was created by the order n° 79-114 of May15, 1979. It replaced the Directorate of Customs and Excises. From 1980 to 1989, it was ruled by the Belgian Cooperation and by the European Economic Community; and by France from 1985 to 1987[26]. Today, it is ruled by local people. The

---

[23] Ibrahima Baba Kaké, *op.cit.*, p.1430.

[24] Mihigo Uguha Michaelle-Brenda, Rapport de stade effectué à l'Office des Douanes et Accises "OFIDA", p.3 in Jean-Paul Esamba Bokel'Ipoka, *Counterfeiting and Piracy in import and export; a strategy of the Democratic Republic of Congo* (Master Thesis), Muenster, University of Muenster, 2008, p.51.

[25] Alain Tenday, *Les procédures douanières en RDC ; expérience du « guichet unique » au poste de Matadi*. Paris, L'Harmattan, 2014, p 45-47.

[26] Jacques-pierre Simbabo-Musubi, rapport de stage effectué à la Direction Générale des Douanes et Accises, Ofida, p.2. in Jean-paul

Decree N°09/043 creates and organises the Directorate General of Customs and Excise. Due to that, it has become a public service with a financial autonomy[27] .

Shortly, the modern history of Congolese customs started after the Berlin conference. Some years later, the Saint Germain agreement authorised Congo to levy duties in export and import. After undergoing some change, to strengthen the struggle against smuggling and levy duties for the public purse in an appropriate way, MOBUTU signed an order which granted this customs its autonomy. Hence, the DRC customs became Office of Customs and Excise, in French Office des Douanes et Accises (OFIDA)[28] on May 15, 1979.

As an Office, its customs policy was mainly embodied in customs tariff and legislation. The tariff used to change from time to time due to the government trade and economic policy as worldwide. Despite the tariff change, the Decree of January 29th, 1949 remained the main legislation applicable for the DRC customs until the promulgation of the New code in 2010.

However, it should be noted that as a developing country, the fiscal role in the DRC customs for the state budget is crucial. That is why, for different reasons, the government decided to change the status of this office into the Directorate General of Customs and Excise[29].

As a Directorate General, it is under the supervision of the Ministry of Finances. Inspite of the change of its

---

Esamba Bokel 'Ipoka, *Counterfeiting and Piracy in import and export ; a strategy of the Democratic Republic of Congo* (Master thesis), Muenster, University of Muenster, 2008; p.51.

[27] Déo Rugwiza Magera, Directeur Général in *Revue des douanes congolaises*, n° 006 octobre 2010, p.5.

[28] The acronym in French, Office des Douanes et Accises.

[29] In French, Direction Générale des Douanes et Accises (DGDA).

status, this Directorate General keeps its administrative and financial autonomy and its structures are alike [30].

[30] Mubibya Silutala, Directeur des Ressources Humaines, l'incidence du démembrement des provinces de la République Démocratique du Congo sur les activités douanières ; 10ème session des Directeurs Centraux et Provinciaux ; juillet 2015, pp2-3.

CHAPTER 2

THE BASICS OF CUSTOMS POLICY

This chapter is all about the basic principles of customs policy : definition, sources and roles, just to name a few.

A. PROBLEMATIC DEFINITION OF CUSTOMS POLICY

It is well known that each problem has a given solution in a given situation. However, in case there is no solution in the matter, it becomes problematic. It is the same case with customs policy definition as shown hereafter.

Let us define both "customs" and "policy" to understand what the two words mean once together.

"Customs" is different from "custom" which means an accepted way of behaving or of doing things in a society or a community"[31]. Here, it is about customs, in French, "douane" although some people agree that "douane" in French is the administration but "douanes" are taxes and duties.

The Revised Kyoto Convention defines "customs" as the Government Service which is responsible for the administration of customs laws and the collection of duties and taxes and which also has the responsibility for the

[31] Sally Wehmeiere, *op.cit.*, p.899.

application of other laws and regulations relating to the importation, exportation movement or storage of goods"[32].

Concerning "**Policy**", the Oxford Learner's Dictionary considers it as a "plan of action agreed or chosen by a political party, a business, etc.

It is a principle that you believe in that influences how you behave, a way in which you usually behave. It is not politics; "the activities involved in getting and using power in public life."[33]

In **Ndengese** cultures or in some other traditional African ones, the words "**politique"**, "**politike**", meaning "**policy**" stands for conspiracy or plot against someone.

After defining **Customs** and **Policy** apart in the previous lines, let us see what "**Customs Policy**" means.

A lot of authors attempted to define **Customs Policy**. Mention can be made of BLINOW, KARPINSKI, CZSYSOWICH, BOZYK, ROSATI, TRZECIAKOWSKI, BUDNIKOWSKI, ZIELINSKA-GLEBOCKA[34], KIMPEMENE. CZSYSOWICH[35] quotes many polish economists who consider customs policy to equal tariff. Mention can be made of: KARPINSKI, BOZYK, ROSATI, TRZECIAKOWSKI, BUDNIKOWSKI, ZIELINSKA-GLEBOCKA.

---

[32] World Customs Organisation, Revised Kyoto Convention, General Annex guidelines, Brussels,2000, p.2.

[33] Sally Wehmeiere, *op.cit.*

[34]Wieslaw Czyzowicz, Customs Policy Module-Theoretical approach, Master of Customs Administration course, University of Muenster, Germany, May 15-16, 2008, p.22.

[35] Wieslaw Czyzowicz, Customs Policy Module-Theoretical approach, Master of Customs Administration course, University of Muenster, Germany, May 15-16, 2009, p.14.

Even some Congolese officers in the customs training which occurred in Kinshasa in 2007 used to define customs Policy as "**tariff**".

After being through their definitions, we conclude that **customs policy** is defined either in terms of national economy, methods and instruments, customs control, payment of duties, movement from central economy to the market economy, as tariff or in terms of international exchanges and trade policy.

That is why, following their definitions, we do not find any one accepted by all of them. This is the reason why, we consider the issue of customs policy definition as problematic.

CZSYSOWICH brings a strong argument to prove that there is no appropriate definition of customs policy so far. He defines customs policy as the whole of actions undertaken by the State or international organisation and its bodies in conjunction with solving discrepancies (conflicts, contradictions, inconsistencies), promotion and protection of the interests of the given country or member states of economic integration groups (single market in the case of a customs union) in international trade in goods by means of establishing of autonomous standards and legal regulations or by means of acceptance of international standards arising from agreements (pacts, treaties or conventions) as well as the implementation of such into the social and economic life of the country in order to ensure the supremacy of own interests over other public interests.

In our view, **Customs policy** is a set of provisions, laws, or measures based on business, regional and international communities, government policy, society needs related to trade and which are applied by the customs administration or any regional or international group to solve conflicts in trade in goods.

B. OBJECTS OF CUSTOMS POLICY

First of all, it would be very crucial to specify what we mean by an **object**. An object is the domain or field of application of any science. That is to say, if we want to consider customs policy as science, two elements are taken into account namely, its object and its method. Here, our emphasis is on the domain of customs policy. The object of customs policy is to solve conflicts which can arise in trade in goods.

C. ELEMENTS OF CUSTOMS POLICY

The following can be considered as the customs policy elements:

1) Activities conducted by the state or an international organization; e.g an economic integration organisation-free trade association or customs union.
2) Multifaceted activities undertaken by entities that work together to form and carry out customs policy (parliament, other legislative bodies or executive authorities, their rights and obligations as well as the rights and obligations of entities carrying out foreign trade.
3) Legal regulations of an autonomous or international nature.

Dispute settlement of interests of a social and economic nature of countries or member states of integration groups associated with the protection and interests such, i.e their supremacy in the context of peaceful international relations associated with the trading of goods[36].

D. SOURCES OF CUSTOMS POLICY

There is a Ndengese saying, "Bapanoka losi opeye bote". It means, we never drink water of any river we do not know its source. The proverb implies that in former times Ndengese people used to drink water from the river. To do so, it was an obligation for the population to know whereby that river or stream started. It means, we never rely on the person or anything we do not know or not talk about anything we are not well informed about.

To comply with this proverb, it would be a big mistake for us to talk about Customs policy, without saying a word on its sources.

Yet, it is known that man is the engine or centre of all activities. Then, Customs policy takes its sources from those activities.

In other words, customs policy is based on human activities or interests which are related to goods, commodities, or to everything for sale or purchase produced by mankind or humanity.

Customs policy sources may be spreaded into 3 categories: economic, legal and international sources.

I. Economic sources

They comprise:

1) Promotion of national business (scale of market):

[36] Wieslaw Czyzowicz, Customs Policy Module-Theoretical approach, Master of Customs Administration course, University of Muenster, Germany, May 15-16, 2008, p.20.

Customs policy should be designed in a way that governments create industries to produce more goods and sell them with lower prices in wholesales. This situation will be beneficial for both industries, and population in that industries will increase their gain and develop other markets. This is very important in African countries whereby the informal trade is current. Once this trade is under the government control, in somehow it can contribute to the country development.

2) Protection of national values (life, health, cultural heritage, etc.):

A good customs policy should take into account the protection of population life, health against dangerous products such as drugs, products of tobacco, etc.

protection of population life and health

-In 2003, there was "a pathogenic avian influenza (H5N1) or bird flu in poultry which began in South-East Asia". To face this challenge, countries banned the meat import from that part of the world. Customs applied the decision. [37]

-On May 29, 2015, Cameroon customs officers seized at the Port of Douala, 18600 CREAM LEMONVATE tubes bearing the words "MADE IN ITALY" imported from China. These counterfeit products were prohibited by the Cameroonian Government.

[37] Ulrich Meiser, Reader, I protection of Health, II Nairobi convention, III johannesburg conventions, World Customs Organisation, compliance and facilitation Directorate Enforcement, 2008, p. 2.

Consumption of drugs

As said Michel Danet, "drugs trafficking is an extremely damaging international phenomenon, adversely affecting all nations, but particularly impacting on those societies and people who are vulnerable to exploitation by organized criminal groups"[38].

Tobacco products

To comply with the World Health Organisation requirements in response to the growing international illicit trade in tobacco products which poses a serious threat to public health, customs has to apply the protocol to eliminate illicit trade in these products which was adopted by consensus on 12th November 2012 at the fifth session of the Conference of the parties (COP) to the WHO FCTC (Seoul, Republic of Korea, 12th-17th November 2012),which addresses means of countering illicit trade in tobacco products, a key aspect of a comprehensive tobacco control policy[39].

The Protocol invites parties, to share information according to domestic law, on tobacco control in import, export, transit, tax-paid and duty-free sales and quantity or value of production of tobacco, tobacco products or manufacturing equipments[40].

Cultural heritage: cultural heritage can be defined as a legacy which is transmitted from generation to generation. It relates to people customs, identity, behaviours, etc. The

---

[38] Michel Danet, Foreword WCO Annual Report 2004 in World Customs Organisation, Compliance and Facilitation Directorate Enforcement, 2008, p. 2.

[39] World Health Organisation, *Protocol to eliminate illicit trade in Tobacco products*, World Health Organisation, Avenue Appia20, 1211 Geneva 27, Switzerland, 2013, p. 1.

[40] *Ibidem*, Article 21, p. 27.

Unesco Convention defines Cultural Property as property which, on religious or secular grounds, is specifically designated by each State as being of importance for archaeology, prehistory, history, literature, art or science and which belongs to the following categories: rare collections and specimens of fauna, flora, minerals and anatomy[41].

This Convention (Artilcle 12) also sustains that to ensure the protection of their cultural property, the States Parties to this Convention shall respect the cultural heritage within the territories for the international relations of which they are responsible, and shall take all appropriate measures to prohibit and prevent the illicit import, export and transfer of ownership of cultural property in such territories [42]. However, the Nairobi convention (Article 12.c) asks to maintain relations with the other international organisations concerned and, in particular, with the competent bodies of the United Nations, with UNESCO and with the International Criminal Police Organisation (Interpol), as regards to action against illicit traffic in narcotic drugs and psychotropic substances, and action against illicit traffic in works of art, antiques and other cultural property[43].

3. Protection of balance of payment (fair competition): when talking about balance of payment, what comes first in mind is globalisation of economy via export and import. It is somehow the trade liberalisation idea developed by

---

[41] Unesco Convention on the means of prohibiting and preventing the illicit import, export and transfer of ownership of cultural property, Article 1, Paris, November 14, 1970.

[42] Ibidem, Article 12.

[43] World Customs Organisation, International Convention on Mutual administrative Assistance for the prevention, investigation and repression of customs offences, Nairobi, 9June 1977, Rue du Marché, 30 B-1210 Brussels, 1999, Article 12.

RICARDO which means that nations are requested to specialize in products in which they have comparative advantages to trade. As shown in the first chapter devoted to the DRC while talking about economic aspect, it is very important for this country which is a geological scandal to specialise in different products such as: cobalt, copper, diamonds, etc to trade with different partners, why not to transform this comparative advantage into competitive one.

4. Protection of infantile industry: this is the economic role played by customs. Let us explain this issue via the following cases:

CASE 1 : In 2009, the Cameroonian customs made some seizures of containers candles and counterfeit matches from China at the Douala Port. It is an eloquent illustration of the fact that counterfeiting and piracy are major obstacles to the development of industry. In this case, goods seized to be dumped on the markets of the sub region mainly in Chad and the Central African Republic, constituted unfair competition for UNALOR company based in Cameroon.

CASE 2 : PILCAM. It is another Cameroonian factory which manufactures batteries with trade mark “HELLENS”. This mark is counterfeited in China. To challenge unfair competition from counterfeiters, on May 29, 2015 during the physical inspection of the container N° TLCU549605/7 from China, operational services of Cameroonian Customs based at the Douala Port, seized 89 cartons of counterfeit batteries "HELLESSENS" bearing words "MADE IN CAMEROON" by PILCAM. Inside these cartons were found 2,400 pieces for a total of 213,600 batteries concealed in cardboard boxes without insignia.

II. National legal sources

They comprise national constitution as a base for legal creation and protection of national customs policy, principal rights for legal and individual persons to free development economic activity not only in the country but also on international market, laws and ordinances. Examples include: Acts on economic activity, law on foreign trade, tax and customs laws, national customs Tariffs, administrative law, implementing provisions, ordinances on certificates requirements for customs clearances[44].

III. International legal sources

They relate to different agreements, treaties, conventions which are signed by states. e.g : Revised Kyoto Convention (RKC), World Trade Organisation (WTO), World Health Organisation (WHO), etc.

As previously said, the scope of Customs Policy is international trade in goods whereby arise conflicts. That is why, referring to the influential sources quoted above, stakeholders involved in this trade are obliged to harmonize and unify their policy in order to speak in one word and play their game well. To comply with that situation, the World Customs Organisation as the only one international organisation in charge of customs matters cooperating with different organisations involved in trade in goods, has designed different instruments and tools such as the Revised Kyoto Convention (RKC), the Frame work of Standards Safe (FOS), the Harmonised System (HS), the Customs Enforcement Network (CEN), etc. For example, the calculation of customs valuation based on the

[44] Wieslaw Czyzowicz Ph.D. Customs Policy Module-Legal and Practical Approach, Master of Customs Administration Course, University of Muenster, Germany, May15-16, 2008, pp,6-8.

GATT Article VII and which is applied by all the World Customs Organisation members, shows how the WTO has an influence on customs matters. So, while designing their customs policies customs should consider these tools and other international organisations quoted above provisions which have influence on trade in goods.

In the case with the DRC, SADC, COMESA, ECCAS, etc. are also very important to be considered while elaborating Customs Policy.

E. FUNCTIONS OF CUSTOMS POLICY

In general, the functions of customs policy are the following: promotional, protective, preferential, fiscal, retorsion and adaptation to the WCO, WTO and GATT 94 norms and standards. Let us consider each of them.

I. Promotional function

It means in fact that, in exportation, taxes do not exist. It is an international accepted situation zero duties because the country of destination will apply duties on imported goods. However, the state has its power to impose taxes and duties for fiscal, economic reasons.

So, during exportation, customs policy plays an important role and is one of the best means of the industry development in that there is absence of taxes and duties or others. It is proper to say that in the case of inward and outwards procedures, producers and traders are granted special procedures which have economic impact on companies or industries[45].

[45] World Trade Organisation, the legal texts, *The results of the Uruguay round of multilateral trade negotiations*, GATT Secretariat, 1994, p.437.

In other words, in the second Republic Zaire, the IVECO company used to import goods in conventional regime CKD (complete knock down) because the company got a special regime which exempted it from customs duties. The reason behind was, imported spares contributed to the development of IVECO Company in the country.

II. Protective function

Customs policy has the mission to protect the nation, people, companies especially infant industries against everything working to their detriment, using autonomous or conventional tariff and non-tariff, including prohibitions, restrictions, ban of turnover, quotas, ceilings, etc.

Coming back to the IVECO example, the protective function applies as well in that conventional regime was granted to IVECO infant industry, to protect it and the Congolese workers'job.

Another case is that Congolese textile company named UTEXAFRICA faced unfair competition from super Soso manufacturers and other textile products. As response to that situation, the DRC Government imposed higher taxes on imported similar textile products.

III. Preferential function

Customs policy is an important instrument to grant industries, companies, in short different partners preferential regimes. That is, lower price or zero one following the agreement signed on this issue.

Let us consider the following examples:

- Preferential rules of origin between China and African Least developed countries

In 2004, to help the African least developed countries, China signed preferential tariffs with them. The list of some products originating from Africa was sent to China. Once these products arrived there, customs duties could not be levied on the goods listed.

- **Cotonou Agreement**: To help African and Caraibe countries, European Union signed the Cotonou Agreement. It is a treaty between the European Union (EU) and the African, Caribbean and Pacific Group of States (ACP countries). It was signed in June 2000 in Cotonou, Benin by 78 ACP countries. Two principles of Cotonou Agreement are related to the issue. They are trade preference and Generalized System of Preference"[46].

Customs policy allows the administration to apply preferential tariffs rates, preferential rules of origin, suspensions, tariffs quotas, tariffs ceilings (…) whenever necessary.

IV. Fiscal function

This is the major function which concerns developing countries where by customs revenues are very important for the public purse. It is the case with Central Africa Customs administrations which depend on the Ministry of Finances. However, due to its sovereignty, the State is free to elaborate its customs policy to levy duties and taxes on export, import and excise duties or to impose any provision on that issue applying autonomous tariffs rates, countervailing duties, agricultural duties and antidumping duties.

---

[46] https://en.wikipedia.org/wiki/cotonou_Agreement. Accessed on 22 June 2015.

V. Retorsion function

Customs policy is a very good instrument since it gives the state or the government the right to impose discriminatory tariffs and non-tariffs measures in case and whenever it is necessary especially once the originating goods are discriminated in the country of the destination.

VI. Adaptation international norms and standards

To avoid conflicts on the ground with different partners while applying laws, any state customs policy must take into account the norms and standards established by international organizations such as WCO, WTO, etc[47].

F. INSTRUMENTS OF CUSTOMS POLICY

Many people use to mistake customs policy for customs law or customs administration. In this context, both customs law and customs administration are customs policy instruments.

It is therefore worth important displaying the role of each of these instruments.

I. Customs laws

There is a lot of discussion surrounding customs law. For some authors especially in Poland, it should be treated as a part of administrative law, for others, customs law is a part of finance, commercial or economic law; in most recent legal literature mostly in Russia, it appears to be an independent discipline of law[48].

---

[47] There is no need to say a word on WTO and GATT 94 since these issues are tackled in the third chapter especially the part devoted to valuation.

[48] Professor Drwillo defines Customs law as "a set of legal regulations, i.e., legislative and executive provisions regulating the

The Revised Kyoto Convention considers customs law as the statutory and regulatory provisions relating to the importation, exportation, movement or storage of goods, administration and enforcement of which are specially charged to the customs, and regulations made by the customs under their statutory powers[49].

Methodologically, Customs law, just like Customs policy, is not precisely defined in either customs doctrines or literature regarding this object.

In this work, Customs law is considered as legal provisions made and which are applied by any customs service or regional grouping to regulate trade in goods. Customs law being defined, let us say something about customs legislation and customs code.

Concerning the act of 9th January of 1997, CZYSOWICH argues that customs code, is of fundamental significance to the whole sphere of foreign commodities trade. For him, the Customs Code, together

---

principles and methods of importing goods into the customs area of a given country as well as export from the given customs territory. The object of the regulations are also the rights and obligations of people importing and exporting goods abroad as well as the rights and obligations of customs authorities. However, the context of customs law provisions indicates that these are legal regulations regarding commodities trade with foreign country.

International commerce of commodities or more precisely, international trade of goods. Therefore, in order to define the precise, i.e. very narrow material and not social aspect, object of customs law regulations; it is much more appropriate to talk about international trade in goods instead of international commerce in general. Customs law within this object matter regulates the mutual relationships between customs authorities and entities involved in international trade of commodities

Drwillo in Ewas and others, *Customs policy. Economics, Laws and Practice*, 2014, p.29.

[49] World Customs Organisation, Revised Kyoto Convention, General Annex guidelines, 2000, p.3.

with the implementing provisions, constitute a group of normative acts, which for methodological purposes can be called customs legislation[50].

Functions of customs law

According to the direction of foreign commodities trade, customs law functions are: export, import and transit; and as far as economic goal are concerned, customs law functions are: protective, promotional and fiscal[51].

Direction of foreign commodities

Export: customs law regulates trade in goods in export. Customs law regulates how goods leaving the country A can reach safely the country B. it stipulates that when goods leave the country A to enter the country B, they must be assigned to export declaration.

Import: customs law regulates trade in goods in import. It regulates how goods coming from the country x enter safely the country Z. It means, the customs law stipulates that when the country z imports goods from the country x, the goods concerned must be assigned to import declaration in the country z.

Transit: customs law regulates trade in goods in transit. It regulates how goods leaving the country A for Z pass via the country x safely and reach Z. Customs law talks about freedom of transit for such goods[52]. That is, such goods (including baggage), and also vessels and other means of transport, shall be deemed to be in transit across the territory of a contracting party when the passage

---

[50] Wieslaw Czyzowich in Etwa and others, *Customs policy economics law and practice*, Jan Brodzinski, 2014, p. 27.
[51] *Ibid*, pp. 38-42.
[52] World Trade Organisation GATT, The legal texts, the results of the Uruguay Round of multilateral trade Negociations, Article V, p.429.

across such territory, with or without trans-shipment, warehousing, breaking bulk, or change in the mode of transport, is only a portion of a complete journey beginning and terminating beyond the frontier of the contracting party across whose territory the traffic passes. Traffic of this nature is termed in this article "traffic in transit" "There shall be freedom of transit through the territory of each contracting party, via the routes most convenient for international transit, for traffic in transit to or from the territory of other contracting parties…".[53]

In our view, in practice, even in transit, members can inspect any suspicious goods if necessary and if their legislations allow them to do so since states are sovereign or independent.

Economic goal

Protective: customs law is an instrument used to protect the society, the infant industry, etc. For instance, to promote local industries, the Zairian government granted economic regimes to different industries[54]. To prevent the population from consuming chickens from Turkey, supposed to have contaminated the bird flu virus, the government of the DRC banned the import of these chickens seized at Pointe Noire in Congo[55].

Promotional: customs law is the tool used to promote the local industry by means of economic regimes for example[56].

Fiscal: customs policy is the appropriate tool used by customs administration to levy duties on imported goods[57].

---

[53] ibidem p 44.
[54] See Iveco.
[55] See Social and economic roles of customs.
[56] See economic role of customs.
[57] See fiscal role of customs.

The DRC has imposed export tax on mineral resources such as: diamond, copper, cobalt, etc.

Security: it is the customs major function in the 21st century. For this reason, the third chapter is devoted to security.

II. Customs administration

Customs administration is an official department or service which is in charge of levying duties on imported goods. In some countries, customs administration perceives these duties even on some exported ones. In countries whereby the Department or official service is also in charge of excise duties, customs is named Department of customs and excise, Directorate General of customs and excise, etc. It is the case with the DRC Directorate General of Customs and Excise, the Belgium Directorate General of Customs and Excise, and the General Department of Customs and Excise of Cambodia, etc.

An **excise duty or excise tax** (sometimes called a special excise duty) is "an inland tax on the sale, or production for sale, of specific goods or a tax on a good produced for sale, or sold, within a country or licenses for specific activities"[58].

However, for some others, "Customs Administration can be considered as the official organisation responsible for collecting taxes on goods coming into a country and preventing illegal goods from being brought in"[59].

Accordingly, customs administration is an official service, department or directorate which is in charge of

[58] https://en.wikipedia.org/wiki/Excise.Accessed on 02.09.2015.

[59] Collins.inhttp://dictionary.reverso.net/English. Accessed on 02 September 2015.

implementing the country or regional organisation trade in goods policy.

Customs administration role, responsibility and business

When we speak of customs role or responsibility in the 21st century, we mean the way it can perform its job. For some of them, it is revenue collection. For others economic role, security (…). In Australia for example, it is border security, security measures.

In most countries, customs is responsible for implementing a wide range of government policies, spanning areas as diverse as revenue collection, enforcement of trade agreements, interdiction of narcotics, prevention of terrorism, protection of cultural heritage and enforcement of intellectual property laws. Any customs administration will have multiple roles to play, including revenue collection and border protection. In addition, with mounting pressure from international trading community to minimise Government intervention in commercial transactions, there is a growing expectation for customs authorities worldwide to place an increasing emphasis on the facilitation of trade[60].

Customs is given the role to reflect the government policy. That is, the government designs the policy to be implemented by customs. So, Customs administration is one of the best tools to implement customs policy in that it allows the country to compete internationally in trade in goods by granting international security on that issue. Within customs administration, there are services which apply integrity, simplification of customs procedures or formalities, post audit control (…) for goods better

[60] Harrisson, Customs Management, theory and practice, University of Muenster, Matser of Customs Policy and Customs Administration, lectures notes prepared for the University of Munster, 2007. P.47.

transactions. It is proper to say that to implement customs policy, customs administration plays the following roles: fiscal, economic, social, external statistics, security, etc. let us consider each role.

Fiscal: it is the traditional role of customs; customs is in charge of levying duties on imported goods and in some countries like the DRC even in exported ones. This is the role of customs since ages, especially in developing countries where by customs depend on the Ministry of Finances. It is the case with countries like: Democratic Republic of Congo, Cameroon, Congo, Gabo n, Central African Republic, Chad, etc.

Economic: It is the mission which relates to the protection of the infant industry. It is the case with developed countries like European ones.

Social: Customs has the social mission to prevent people from consuming the illicit trade products (counterfeit goods, drugs or any dangerous goods for health), etc[61].

External statistics: being at borders, Customs is also in charge of elaborating external statistics. This task is very important for the elaboration of the balance of payment.

Security: This is the most important role of customs in the 21st century in that, without security, there is no way for customs to fulfill other roles quoted above. It is the case with the USA where by customs belongs to the Homeland Security Department.

According to DEWULF[62] the responsibilities of customs continue to evolve. Customs administrations are now increasingly regarded as "the key border agencies"

---

[61] See customs policy economic sources.

[62] Dewulf and José B. Sokol, *Customs modernization*, Handbook World Bank, 2005, p.3.

responsible for all transactions related to issues arising from border crossings of goods and people. Some of these functions are undertaken in close cooperation with national agencies.

In our opinion, DEWULF view complies with the third pillar of the WCO Framework of Standard Safe which emphasises on such cooperation at borders and which is deeply developed in the fourth chapter.

G. CUSTOMS POLICY CREATORS

By customs policy creators we mean, customs makers. That is, different bodies which trigger customs policy. They are classified at two different levels:

I. National level

1) Business and social lobbies (branch and regional, e.g. chambers of commerce and industry, professional lobbyists, trade unions, other social groups-ecologists, etc.).

As said in the previous chapter, Chambers of commerce and industry and some other institutions play an important role in trade in goods. Their activities have a big influence on this issue and make them part of customs policy. To levy duties in import, customs needs valuation, tariff and the origin of goods. Chambers of commerce are in charge of issuing the certificate of origin.

2) Legislative bodies (Parliament and regional or local legislative bodies-originators of legal environment-constitution, laws, acts, ordinances, etc.)

It is well known that legislative bodies are institutions, structures which make, validate countries laws. They make Customs policy for the simple reason that Customs

Policy embodies also laws related to trade in goods, made by the bodies quoted above.

3) Executive bodies (President, governments, national, regional and local).

As ruling bodies, Executive ones make customs policy since they have power. Their speeches, decisions are instruments or tools used to make customs policy. Eg. The DRC customs reform and modernisation 2003 programme was based on the Government triennial plan.

4) Customs administration (Customs service) enforcement the customs law.

As one of the best tool to implement customs policy, customs administration makes it as well. In this case, it is considered like the guardian, heart or soldier in that customs administration receives instructions from the Head of army which is the government to implement customs policy.

However, the difference lies on that in the army, the soldier has no word to say to his Head. But customs administration has in that it suggests laws which are adopted by the executive bodies to make customs policy. e.g The DRC customs reform and modernisation 2003 based on the trienal planning was made by customs administration experts and submitted to the government of republic.

5) Courts (administrative, appeal, local and national, interpretation of customs law and

Courts make customs policy in that they are in charge of judging conflicts related to trade in goods in case parties cannot reach an agreement. During trials, laws and provisions are legal references for judges on this endavour. Furthermore, Courts decisions adopted at the end of some trials can be drawn as lessons for future situations and become laws to solve trade in goods conflicts. It is the case with England where by the law is not developed in written basis but on the basis of the court judgements.

II. International level

1) Intergovernmental economic organisations WTO/GATT, WCO, UN, WB and IMF, regional economic integration, EU.

Intergovernmental organisations make customs policy in that they create provisions, instruments, tools that affiliated members embody in their national trade in goods policy. It is one of the reasons why customs administrations have different priorities but once at the border, they apply the same instruments like valuation method, based on GATT Article VII, freedom of transit GATT Article 8, The Revised Kyoto convention, etc.

2) Other intergovernmental organisations UNCTAD, UNIDO, WIPO, NATO, SADC, etc.

Intergovernmental organisations make customs policy since Members belonging to them comply with their provisions or laws which are uniform to avoid discrepancies in trade in goods law application by members[63].

3) Business international organisation (NGOS) ICC, branch and regional business association, e.g. CONFIAD[64].

---

63 See also (1).

64 Wieslaw Czyzowicz, Customs Policy Module-legal and practical Approach, Master of Customs Administration Course, University of Muenster, Germany, May 15-16, 2007, p.9.

The influence of business international organisation was dealt with while talking about the definition of customs policy. What is said about other organisations concerns Business international organisation as well.

H. MEASURES OF CUSTOMS POLICY

We distinguish two groups of customs policy measures. They are: tariffs policy and non-tariff policy.

I. Tariff policy

By "tariff", we mean, the document which displays duties or taxes to be levied per products. It is composed of: the list of products and the duty rate to levy.[65] So, tariff policy refers to the elaboration of customs tariff nomenclature. That is, (a) the "Harmonised Commodity Description and Coding System", referred to as the "Harmonised System", meaning the Nomenclature comprising the headings and subheadings and their related numerical codes, the Section, Chapters and Subheading Notes and the General Rules for the interpretation of the Harmonised System. It is (b) the World Customs Organisation nomenclature established under the legislation of a Contracting Party for the purposes of levying duties of Customs on imported goods[66].

Tariff is important since it helps simplification of customs procedures, the use of a common language which is accepted in trade at the international level (...). Tariff, origin and valuation are key elements for the calculation of customs duties and taxes.

---

[65] Ecole des Douanes de Neuilly sur seine, Présentation de l'espèce tarifaire, p.3.
[66] World Customs Organisation, Convention on Harmonised System.

One can argue in one word that Tariff policy measures are for fiscal, economical, social and security purposes.

Fiscal: tariff is an instrument to levy duties on imported goods.

Economical: tariff is used to protect the industry. Achim ROGMANN sustains that GATT Article 18 permits Developing Countries to raise tariffs and use other means to protect the so-called infant industries[67].

Social: tariff is also used to protect the society.

Security: Tariff can help identify strategic goods which are used to manufacture weapons of mass destructions.

Tariff policy is divided into two groups namely, tariffs rates and tariffs measures.

Tariffs rates are those applied on imported goods. There are three basic types of tariffs: **advalorem** (percentage of the value), **specific** (flat tax per imported item) and **mixed** which combines both advalorem and specific. In the nomenclature, they are advalorem, i.e expressed in percentage."[68] E.g. the DRC customs tariff 2003 rate for vegetables chapter 07 and fruits chapter 8 are 10% apart from potatoes seeds 5% and fruits 20%. On top of that, Achim ROGMANN sustains that the criterion used for calculating the tariff can either be specific (such as weight, quantity, size) or specific value and /or a mixture of the both.

Tariffs measures comprise tariffs preferences General Special Preferential (GSP), Free Trade Area (FTA), lower

---

[67] Achim Rogmann, principles of WTO laws, University of Muenster, Master of customs administration 2008, p. 28.

[68] Achim Rogmann, Customs Valuation Law, the EU Model Brunswick European Law School, August 2008, p.3.

rates, suspensions and tariffs restrictions which are autonomous rates, quotas and ceilings.

II. Non-tariffs policy

It comprises trade prohibitions, that means sanctions and embargoes, and non-tariffs restrictions equal quantity limitations, technical barriers, phitosanitary and veterinary norms, etc.

A part from trade prohibitions and non-tariffs restrictions, non-tariffs policy also comprise safeguard measures which are anti-dumping duties and countervailing ones.

CHAPTER 3

THE SECURITY MISSION OF CUSTOMS

As said in the previous chapter, security is the major function of customs in the 21st century. As far as security is concerned, this chapter tries to go through what the international customs community has done in the matter so far, especially the implementation of Security Programme at the level of World Customs Organisation Secretariat. After being through the Security Programme, we will try to give our view point on the contribution of the UN 1540 and Punta Cana resolutions to the security mission of customs.

According to Stefan Aniszewski[69], it is difficult to find an appropriate definition for security. However, he tries to define security within the framework of customs as the activities performed by the WCO and which relate to border security, facilitation of customs procedures, protection of society, etc.[70]

Accordingly, security is the fact of being in peaceful condition. It is a bit different from safety which relates to the fact of being saved from a deadly situation.

In our view the safety function of customs is related more to the personal side: IPR, consumer protection, etc. Whereas security addresses more overarching issues, such

---

[69] Stefan Aniszewski was the Security Programme Manager at the World Customs Organization until 2016

[70] World Customs Organisation, 35th session of Enforcement Committee (EC) from 29 February to 3 March 2016.

as terrorism, by programmes like Strategic Trade Control Enforcement(STCE).

A. THE IMPORTANCE OF THE SECURITY MISSION OF CUSTOMS

As said in chapter 2, there is no way for customs to perform its roles perfectly without security. That is, without security there is no way for customs to levy customs and excise duties, to facilitate trade, to protect society, to protect local industry, to fight against fraud, to protect Intellectual Property Rights, to protect environment, to fight against money laundering, to protect cultural heritage, etc.

Some psychologists such as Carl Rogers while dealing with creativity underlined the importance of an encouraging environment that facilitates the person's growth[71]. It is security.

Carl Rogers considers security to be a sine qua none condition for creativity. That is, to perform the job in good conditions. It means, security is very important in a professional area in that, if a person feels secure, he can create, innovate and accomplish his duties in an appropriate way. That is why, security in any job, customs in this case, is mandatory.

On the orther hand, Customs is at borders. It is the filter which controls the movement of goods, people, means of transportation, etc. It means that without customs involvement, the fight against terrorism becomes difficult. That is why, as emphasized by the WCO Security Programme, customs has to play its role as stated in the UN 1540 and Punta Cana resolutions.

---

[71] https://www.the positiveencouraging.global/carl-rogers-and-the-person-ce. Accessed on 2 Juin, 2018.

Being at borders, Customs will control the UN sanctions and embargoes imposed on different states.

B. SECURITY MISSION LEGAL BASIS

The following can be considered as legal basis while talking about security in customs. These are:

- Revised Kyoto Convention
- UN 1540 Resolution
- WCO Punta Cana Resolution
- Counter-terrorism strategy

Let us take a look at each legal instrument:

I. The Revised Kyoto Convention

The Revised Kyoto Convention, chapter 5[72], recommends that customs should use security. In our view, it seems to be not clear in the way customs has to put in place that security; the Convention just recommends that customs should refer to national laws[73].

II. The UN 1540 Resolution

Today, nobody can deny terrorism exists. All continents around the world are victimised by this scourge. We have Boko Haram, Al-quaida in Islamic Maghreb (Aqmi) and other terrorist groups in Sahel which are active in Africa and kill people in Nigeria, Cameroon, Niger, Chad, Mali, Burkina Faso, Ivory Coast..., Al Shebab killing in Kenya, Somalia (...) in the Eastern part of Africa, ADF NAlu and several army groups killing in

---

[72] World Customs Organization, Kyoto Convention, General Annex Guidelines, 2000, p3-10).

[73] World Customs Organisation, Revised Kyoto Convention, General Annex guidelines, chapter 5 2000, pp. 3-9.

the Democratic Republic of Congo in Central Africa, Islamic states (ISIL) Da'esh, Al-quaida killing in France, Belgium, Germany in Europe, in Asia, in the United States of America, in Russia, Afghanistan, Pakistan, etc.

To combat terrorism, on 28 April 2004, the United Nations Security Council unanimously adopted the Resolution 1540. In its Chapter VII, the United Nations Charter imposes binding obligations on all states to take and enforce « effective measures » to prevent proliferation of nuclear, chemical, or biological weapons and their means of delivery, including, inter alia, export, transshipment, transit and border controls and law enforcement to block illicit trafficking of related materials.[74]

Since the fight against terrorism cannot succeed without customs involvement at borders, the UN Resolution is constructed in a way that it is only customs who can do the things included in the following operative paragraphs:

paragraph 3.c: establish effective border controls and law enforcement efforts to detect, deter, prevent and combat... the illicit trafficking and brokering in such items ;

- paragraph 3.d: establish, develop, review and maintain appropriate effective national export and trans-shipment controls over such items[75].

After the UN had adopted the Resolution 1540, in order to help Member administrations apply this resolution, the WCO endorsed the Punta Cana Resolution presented hereafter.

---

[74] World Customs Organisation, Strategic Trade Control Enforcement(STCE), International legal frameworks and regimes to govern strategic trade, p.14.

[75] *Ibidem*, p.15.

III. The Punta Cana Resolution

On December 2015, within the framework of Security Programme in relation to the UN Resolution quoted above, the WCO adopted the Punta Cana Resolution. As opposed to the Revised Kyoto Convention which seems not to clarify how customs will implement security while performing its job, the Punta Cana resolution seems to be more specific in that, it spells out the security function of customs in general which includes the fight against proliferation of WMD. It invites customs authorities to include security as part of their mandate and functions, where appropriate, by including security in their strategic plans, endorses close cooperation at national, regional and international level between customs authorities and between customs and other law enforcement authorities in relation to information exchange and investigations, invites customs authorities to use the full range of detection and investigate techniques, including risk profiling, etc[76].

IV. Counter-terrorism strategy

Shortly, according to Security WCA 2016, the counter-terrorism strategy has been implemented in 2016, to enhance the capacity of customs administrations to manage border security related to threats.

C. THE WCO SECURITY PROGRAMME

The World Customs Organisation activities in the issue of security are embodied in the following five areas:

---

[76] World Customs Organisation, Punta Cana Resolution, Resolution of the Policy Commission of the World Customs Organisation on the role of Customs in the security context, December 2015, p.3. See also World Customs Organisation Strategic Trade Control Enforcement (STCE), components of national strategic Trade Control Systems p.4.

- **Global Shield (GS)**: Global Shield was first a project implemented by the World Customs Organisation in partnership with International Criminal Police Organisation (INTERPOL) and the United Nations Office on Drugs and Crime (UNODC) and became a programme later. It aims at combating Improvised Explosives Devices (IEDs) employed by terrorists around the world and which are manufactured using precursor chemicals. The Global Shield Programme monitors the following 14 precursor chemicals listed hereafter: Ammoniumm Nitrate, Acetic Anhydride, Acetone, Urea, Aluminium Powder and Flakes, Hydrogen Peroxide, Nitric Acid, Nitromethane, Potassium chlorate, Potassium Nitrate, Potassium Perchlorate, Sodium Nitrate, Calcium Ammoniun Nitrate.[77]

- **Small Arms and Light Weapons (SALW)**: "**Small Arms**" refer to weapons designed for individual use. Ex: handguns, rifles, carbines, sub-machine guns, assault rifles and light machine guns. However, "**Light weapons**" refer to crew served machineguns and high-explosive projectile weapons. Ex: grenade launchers, automatic grenade launchers (…)[78]. According to Security WCA 2016, the SALW project aims at countering the misuse of IEDS identified by the Global Shield Programme.

- **Passenger controls:** today, the fight against terrorism has become a scourge which requires global commitment. The World Customs Organization has understood that to win this fight, there is need for controlling not only materials (circulation of arms, ammunitions, IED precursors), but also people who trigger those actions via their trips, journeys and means of transportation. Since the

---

[77] World Customs Organization, *Global Shield Programme.*

[78] https://en.wikipedia.org/wiki/small-Arms_and_lihgt_weapons. Accessed on 30 May,2018

means of transportation by air is the most used by people and can allow them to commit terrorist attacks, we deem that, it is one of the reasons why, within the framework of its battle against terrorism, the WCO has taken several initiatives among which the identification of passengers to strengthen aviation security. That is, "the passengers control which is supported by the use of Advanced Passenger Information (API) and by Passenger Name Recorder (PNR)"[79].

However, following the *Guide line on passengers*, it should be noted that API involves the capture of a passenger's biography data and other flight details by carrier prior to departure and transmission of details by electronic means to the border control agencies in the destination country. API can act also as a decision making tool that border agencies can employ before a passenger is permitted to board an aircraft. The WCO sees API as a very useful technique to enhance border security.[80]

- **Terrorist financing:** the aim of terrorist financing is to combat illicit trade and money laundering including cash couriers and trade-based money laundering[81].

- **Strategic trade control:** after the adoption of the UN 1540 Resolution and the World Customs Organization Punta Cana one, the WCO Members raised the issue of how they will combat the proliferation of Weapons of Mass Destruction and their related items[82] while performing their jobs on the ground. To respond to that request the WCO initiated some missions of diagnosis at

---

[79] World Customs Organisation, security project for West and Central Africa (Customs counter-terrorism initiative for West and Central Africa). (paper).

[80] World Customs Organisation, Guide line on passengers, pp. 8-9.

[81] *Ibidem.*

[82] World Customs Organisation, Strategic Trade Control Enforcement (STCE), implementation Guide, p.9.

its regions in order to identify different challenges its Members may face on this issue. After identifying those challenges, the WCO has produced the Strategic Trade Control Enforcement Implementation Guide, which was endorsed by its Members.

The guide is a practical assistance related to enforcing strategic trade controls. The Strategic Trade Control Enforcement Implementation Guide provides guidance to WCO Members in the development and review of their Strategic Trade Control Enforcement (STCE) processes and procedures, and provide a framework for training along those lines[83].

For reasons of security and international agreements, strategic goods are considered to be goods not allowed to export, import or transit to certain countries or only under certain conditions. It concerns goods which can be used for military purposes, for both civil and military purposes, or for the production of weapons of mass destruction and/or means of delivery for such weapons[84].The weapons concerned here are those of mass destruction (WMD), conventional weapons and related items involved in the development, production, or use of such weapons and their delivery systems.[85]

---

[83] Ibidem, p9.

[84] https://www.belastingdienst.nl/wps/wcm/connect*bldcontenten /belastingdienst/customs/safetyhealth-economy and environment/cdiu cluster/strategic goods/strategic goods. Accessed on 21 May, 2018.

[85] Weapons of Mass Destructions are: nuclear weapons(NW) designed to cause mass destruction through the explosive release of nuclear energy, chemical weapons(CW)designed to inflict injury such as chocking, blistering, or nervous system malfunction through chemical reactions, biological weapons(BW)designed to employ microorganisms to cause illness in humans, livestock, or crops, radiological weapons(RW) designed to cause illness and mass disruption through the spread of radioactivity,delivery systems include ballistic missiles, cruise missiles, and unmanned aerial vehicles...

However, it should be noted that Strategic Trade Control combines capacity building and operational activities.

The STCE Programme reflects how relevant international legal frameworks and regimes regulate the scene. Members get the opportunity to learn the international commitments made by States to control the export of strategic products, the obligations of these States vis-à-vis the international community, know how these obligations are implemented through national laws, the role of customs to help member states to fight against the proliferation of weapons of mass destruction, etc. Since it combines capacity building and operational activities, what can we suggest to the DRC customs? Some suggestions and lessons to this administration are proposed in our following view point related to the two resolutions mentioned above.

D. OUR VIEW POINT RELATING TO THE CONTRIBUTION OF RESOLUTIONS 1540 AND PUNTA CANA TO THE SECURITY MISSION OF CUSTOMS

As already mentioned, we insist on the fact that security is the customs major function in the 21st century. Before the UN 1540 and the WCO Punta Cana Resolutions one, the World Customs Organisation took different initiatives related to security. The Revised Kyoto Convention for example in its chapter five, recommends customs to use security, the Framework of

---

Related items are materials, equipment and technology covered by relevant multilateral treaties and arrangements, or included on national control lists, which could be used for the design, development, production or use of nuclear, chemical and biological weapons and their means of delivery.

Strategic Trade Control Enforcement(STCE) Training modules,

standards(FOS), recommends the security of supply chain, the Global Shield Programme combats proliferation of IEDCs, etc. In its Security Programme as seen above, the World Customs Organization considers five areas namely, the Global Shield, Small Arms and Light Weapons, Strategic Trade Control Enforcement, Passengers controls and financing terrorism and border security.

To implement these programmes, the WCO refers to different resolutions adopted by the United Nations Security Council.

After being through all these activities and their legal basis, this work deems that the resolution 1540 which has produced the Punta Cana one can be considered like the major text or reference legal basis while dealing with security to date for the following reasons: the Revised Kyoto Convention which is considered like a blue print in terms of customs procedures as said, recommends customs to use security; but in contrast to the UN 1540 and the Punta Cana resolutions , the Revised Kyoto Convention is not specific in the template to follow on this issue. Let us consider the following:

In case of STCE:

To fight against the proliferation of Weapons of Mass Destruction(WMD): customs shall include security in its strategic plan, check whether national laws are likely to help the country to comply with international commitments in order to combat the proliferation of weapons of mass destruction, have a list of strategic products and integrate them into national laws, create a service in charge of strategic goods in customs, strengthen cooperation with companies which produce strategic goods and competent authorities involved in the matters[86].

This book deems that the same framework needs to be revized while dealing with Global Shield, SALW, PNR (…).

IN CASE OF GLOBAL SHIELD

Customs shall include security in its strategic plan, check whether national laws are likely to help the country to combat the circulation of Improvised Explosives Devices (IEDs) employed by terrorists around the world and which are manufactured using precursor chemicals, have a list of 13 precursor chemicals listed hereafter(the list may be updated): Ammoniumm Nitrate, Acetic Anhydride, Acetone, Urea, Aluminium Powder and Flakes, Hydrogen Peroxide, Nitric Acid, Nitromethane, Potassium chlorate, Potassium Nitrate, Potassium Perchlorate, Sodium Nitrate, Calcium Ammoniun Nitrate and integrate them into national laws, create a service dealing with Global Shield in customs, strengthen cooperation with companies, societies which produce precursor chemicals and competent authorities involved in the matters (...).

---

86 World Customs Organisation, Punta Cana Resolution, Resolution of the Policy Commission of the World Customs Organisation on the role of Customs in the security context, December 2015, p.3. See also World Customs Organisation Strategic Trade Control Enforcement.

In case of SALW:

Customs shall include security in its strategic plan, check whether national laws are likely to help the country to comply with international commitments in order to combat the proliferation of SALW, have a list of Small Arms and Lights Weapons and integrate them into national laws, create a service dealing with SALWs in customs, strengthen cooperation with companies, societies which produce SALWs and competent authorities involved in the matters (...).

In case of passengers controls and financing terrorism:

Customs shall include security in its strategic plan, check whether national laws are likely to help the country to comply with international commitments related to Passengers controls and struggle against financing terrorism, have a list of regular passengers and currency seizures data, create a service in charge of passengers movements, strengthen cooperation with air companies, societies and competent authorities involved in the matters (...).

In case of border security:

Customs shall include security in its strategic plan, check whether national laws are likely to help the country to comply with international commitments related to border security, have a list of regular passengers, most currency seizures, goods imported and exported and most regular means of transportation, create a service in charge of frequent passengers movements, most declared goods in import and export, strengthen cooperation with air, sea, road companies, etc., societies and competent authorities(immigration, police, ...) involved in the matters(...).

As far as the UN 1540 and WCO Punta Cana resolutions as reference legal basis in security issues are concerned, since STCE combines both capacity building and operational activities, what can we suggest to the DRC customs? The item below tackles this issue.

E. LESSONS AND SUGGESTIONS TO THE DRC CUSTOMS RELATING TO STCE

Concerning the DRC customs, the STCE programme helps Congolese officers to know the DRC non-proliferation commitments. For reader's information, as a UN member, the DRC has taken the following commitments so far: the Treaty on Non –Proliferation of nuclear Weapons (NPT), the Chemical Weapons Convention (CWC) and the Biological Weapons Convention (BWC)...[87].

As argued in the economic aspect of the DRC in chapter one, the Democratic Republic of Congo is the richest country in the world in terms of ores. In accordance with the UN Resolution 1540 and the WCO Punta Cana resolution, the following suggestions are important for the DRC customs to play its role while fighting the proliferation of weapons of Mass Destructions:

- check whether the Directorate General of Customs and Excise has included security in its strategic plan;
- Check if the DRC has a list of strategic products and if they are integrated into national laws;

[87] World Customs Organisation, Strategic Trade Control Enforcement (STCE), implementation Guide, p.37.

- check whether national laws are likely to help the country to comply with international commitments to combat the proliferation of weapons of mass destruction;
- encourage the DRC customs administration to create a service in charge of strategic goods;
- strengthen cooperation with companies, societies which produce strategic goods and competent authorities involved in the matters.

It should be noted that, the DRC has just adopted a new mineral code, an important instrument on this issue which considers products such as cobalt, germanium, lithium… as strategic.

CHAPTER 4

THE CUSTOMS POLICY OF THE DEMOCRATIC REPUBLIC OF CONGO FROM 2003 to 2010

This chapter relates the way the DRC customs dealt with the trade in goods policy from 2003 to 2010 by implementing the customs reform and modernisation programme which brought a new landscape in this administration. Other aspects related to this policy are discussed as well.

A. CUSTOMS REFORM AND MODERNISATION PROGRAMME

Since ages, the traditional role of customs has always been levying duties for the public purse. Customs also plays an important economic role that is protecting infant industries. It also aims at: protecting the society, intellectual property rights, environment; combating terrorism, fraud, money laundering, illicit trafficking in endangered species, illicit trafficking in cultural heritage; assuring security, etc. In spite of these multiple roles, each customs administration although applying the same instruments and tools at borders, has its priorities. Coming back to the protection of local industry, considering for example countries like Japan which places emphasis on that issue. It is also the case with Western countries. Indeed, in European countries like Germany Intellectual Property Rights issues are very important. In USA or

Canada, security is much concerned. Customs is then incorporated in the homeland Department.

In developing countries, the customs fiscal role remains very crucial for the state budget. In the DRC for example, customs almost contributes about 40% to the state budget. However, while performing their jobs at borders, customs faces some challenges such as: corruption, fraud, lack of appropriate equipment or material, outdated legislations, lack of sufficient trained officers, lack of sufficient cooperation with other stakeholders, jealousy, envy, etc. As result, these challenges keep Customs from performing its job the way, it should do. To address them, by the end of the 20th century, a lot of customs administrations among which the DRC had decided to transform their customs administrations with financial and technical support from international financial institutions and bilateral donors like: World Bank, World Customs Organisation, International Monetary Fund, United Nations Conference on Trade and Development[88].

A lot of literature has been developed on customs reform and modernisation. The International Monetary Fund for example, wrote about customs administration reform and modernisation in Francophone sub-sahara Africa 1995-2000. Dewulf considers the reforms measures themselves covering; management changes; staff related questions such as pay, selection, training, integrity, and corruption, information technology, valuation, experience with pre-shipment inspection; special import regimes; selectivity in pre-and post-release control.[89]

In the previous item, we gave the reason why, different governments had reformed their administrations. By

---

[88] Dewulf and josé B. Sokol, *customs modernisation, Handbook*, World Bank, 2005, p.IX.
[89] Ibidem, p.136.

customs reform and modernisation, we mean the fact of updating customs with new laws, techniques or provisions to help it do the job in an appropriate way and in accordance with modern regulations. That is, the fact of moving from the status quo to adopt new customs management techniques or laws in accordance with the government, the international business community, the society and international community needs. The change or transformation may be at the level of procedures and laws. That is, what this book considers to be the **reform**. But, when the change is done at the level of equipments, it is **modernisation.**

In other words, customs reform are linked to laws and structures changes. Following UN notes, Revised International Kyoto Convention on Simplification and Harmonisation of Customs Procedures is considered as the key international instrument on Customs reform[90]. However, modernisation is connected to technology changes such as the automation of the customs administration.

Reform and modernisation is not only a vector for the introduction of international standards and recommended best practices related to ICT, but also an opportunity for reviewing and aligning Customs procedures to international standards, conventions and other instruments, e.g the Revised Kyoto Convention[91].

There are some cases of reforms and modernisation in Bolivia, Morroco and Philippines[92]. Customs reform and

---

[90] United Nations, *Trade facilitation, part II, Technical Notes on Essential Trade facilitation Measures*, New York and Geneva, 2006, p.42.

[91] Ibidem, p.68.

[92] In Bolivia, customs reform aimed at its total transformation. One of the key elements of the reform was a complete staff renewal designed to rid the service of deeply embedded corruption. In Ghana, it was

modernisation being deeply explained, let us see the specific case of the DRC.

B. CUSTOMS REFORM AND MODERNISATION IN THE DEMOCRATIC REPUBLIC OF CONGO

Dewulf sustains that a successful customs reform requires political commitment and must start with a good diagnosis of the present situation[93].

In the Democratic Republic of Congo, the programme of customs reform and modernization started in 1997 especially with the ruling committee led by the President Managing Director, Juvenal Lufuma Makanda. He implemented the Kin-Aéro single window inside the Tresco warehouse at the N'Djili Airport. Unfortunately, it was burnt due to the 2000 explosion which killed a lot of people among whom customs officers.

Despite that sad situation, upon his nomination as the Head of Customs administration, Albert Kasongo Mukonzo succeeded to implement the Customs reform and modernisation programme 2003 discussed here.[94] The

---

undertaken initially as a case study of reform that would improve the investment climate. However, in Morocco, programme of customs reform and modernization reflected a comprehensive vision and covered all aspects of customs from its organization to its operation. In Philippines, the reform included the use of risk-management techniques, increased emphasis on controls pre-arrival and post-release rather than at the point of entry, and improved of information technology. Morocco and Philippines are the two examples of successful customs Administration modernization. Dewulf and josé B. Sokol, *op.cit.*, p135.

[93] Dewulf, Sokol, *op.cit.*, p.7.

[94] Mwange Muteba, *l'Analyse de l'incidence du Guichet Unique sur les recettes de l'Etat au port de Matadi*, Université Pédagogique Nationale, Kinshassa, p.27.

programme implementation started from 2003 until the arrival of Deo Rugwiza Magera in 2005.

In fact, once Kasongo left his office, he was replaced by Deo Rugwiza Magera who decided to pursue the same programme which has been initiated since 2003, he considered to be a process which aimed at bringing the DRC customs at the level of modern customs 21st Century. According to him, the programme of reform and modernisation helped the DRC customs to maximise revenue and complied with the Revised Kyoto Convention which is incorporated in the Congolese customs code in terms of customs procedures.[95]

Overall, DRC customs reform and modernisation programme includes three areas. They are: simplification and facilitation of customs procedures, optimisation of the mechanism of combating fraud, reorganisation of services and measures programmes[96].

Let us go through each area:

I. Simplification and facilitation of customs procedures

In its policy, the World Trade Organisation places stress on trade liberalisation. To do so, the WTO invites customs which is at borders to simplify and facilitate its customs procedures. That is why, the World Customs Organisation implemented the Revised Kyoto Convention considered as a blue print on facilitation and simplification of customs procedures. To comply with the World Trade Organisation policy on this issue which is incorporated in

---

[95] Deo Rugwiza Magera, in *Notes Explicatives du Système Harmonisé*, 5e éd., Tome1 Sections I-VI, Chapitres1-28, 2012.

[96] Office des Douanes et Accises, Programme de Réforme et Modernisation de l'Office des Douanes et Accises, décembre 2002, pp. 5-7.

the Revised Kyoto Convention, within the frame work of its programme of reform and modernisation the DRC adopted the simplification and facilitation of its customs formalities. The key issues were: the payment of duties, the simplification of customs declarations, the computerisation of procedures, the elaboration of a new customs and excise codes, the reform of tariff, etc.[97]

II. Optimisation of the mechanism of combating fraud

The issue of customs fraud is known worldwide especially in developing countries where it is frequent. To combat this scourge within the framework of its customs reform and modernisation programme, the DRC customs took different measures. The emphasis was put on the following: revision of the services implantation card, redefinition of their staff, best coverage of the territory by a distribution of balanced staff, redeployment of agents to productive jobs in the fight against fraud, Memorandum Of Understanding with the OCC, strengthening cooperation with authorities, development of international Mutual Administrative Assistance and computerisation of customs and excisable procedures (ASYCUDA), etc.[98]

III. Reorganisation of services

The reorganisation of services relates to the general management of the DRC customs. It is the matter to reform these services in a way that they become performant.

---

[97] *Ibidem*, pp 8-17.

[98] *Ibidem*, pp,18-25.

IV. The 2003 programme measures

Those are measures taken to support the programme. The focus is for example on the Congolese customs revue to disseminate information related to the programme, the training of officers, etc.[99].

In our view, the 2003 customs reform and modernisation programme seems to be the customs policy of the DRC from 2003 to 2010 because, customs policy takes into account: government policy, international traders (business community), society and international community. It includes all of the given state's or international economic integration organisation's activities with the aim to solve peacefully conflict of interests in foreign trade of goods, protecting, promoting and providing the superiority of national interests (or common interests in integration organisation) to the public interests of other social groups organised in states and/or trade coalitions.

Customs policy also means creating legal norms and regulations-autonomic or based on international standards (treaties, agreements or conventions) and implementing them into state's own social and economic life[100]. A good customs policy must take into account the social, economic and fiscal functions of customs. As said Keen, "Change is required in four key areas: establishing coherent trade policies and clear supporting legislation, adopting modern, simple procedures, shifting to substantial reliance on self-assessment by tax-payers, supported by movement from physical to post-release controls and ensuring incentive and organizational

---

[99] *Ibidem*, pp26-40.

[100] Wieslaw Czyzowicz, *Customs Policy Module-Theoritical Approach* (Master of Customs Administration Course), University of Muenster, Germany, May15-16, 2008, p. 36.

structures conducive to integrity and effectiveness in customs administration"[101]. Yet, the 2003 programme of reform and modernisation was based on the government triennial programme and embodies customs functions and Keen's key areas.

Let us consider Keen's key areas and see how the 2003 programme complies with some aspects of the reform and modernisation requirements hereafter. The emphasis is mainly on: legislation, automation, tariff, valuation and customs revue.

V. Some key issues of reform and modernisation in the DRC

1. Legislation

Three types of legislations are taken into account in the DRC customs. They are: customs legislation, Excise legislation and connected legislation.

a) Customs legislation

Before and after the independence, the DRC customs only had one legislation known as the 1949 Decree which embodied in total 320 Articles.109 articles related to the Decree and the remaining ones to the Ordinance-law of 1950. So, in spite of changes occurring in different international areas which have a real influence on customs policy, the Decree remained applicable until 2009. Due to the fact that it was no longer updated and could not comply with the current international economic environment, there was a need for the DRC customs to reform it and get a legal text that would be flexible and comply with current realities. So, the DRC customs

---

[101] Michael Keen, *Changing customs; challenges and strategies for the reform of customs administration*, International Monetary Fund, 2003, pp.11-12.

experts worked hard and produced the new customs code to date. Following the national laws, the new code was sent to the parliament for adoption and took time before its promulgation by the President of Republic in 2010.

It should be noted, however, that the implementation of Customs Code in 2010 is one of major achievements while talking about the customs reform and modernisation in the Democratic Democratic Republic of Congo. However, for the simple reason that as this code is based on the Revised Kyoto Convention, it brought a new landscape in terms of customs procedures. The new customs code rejected the Brussels valuation method and took into account valuation according to GATT Article VII; the security of supply chain is strongly emphasised towards the application of framework of standard (SAFE) of the World Customs Organisation (WCO) and on other foreign national codes as well as community. It means, the new code has brought some of the following innovations in terms of simplification and facilitation of customs procedures. Voltaire Mampinda mentioned some of them namely: rights for anyone to accomplish by oneself the acts and customs formalities, and possibility of a goods declaration for customs agent, the automation of customs procedures, protection of intellectual property rights, customs economic regimes, opportunities of free zones and special economic zones on the national territory, Coordination of controls with other public services at the borders, release of the goods in the shortest time possible[102]

b) Excise legislation

The DRC customs comprises two components: customs and excise. Customs is in charge of levying duties and

[102] Voltaire Mampinda, "Facilitation et Simplification des procédures, une réalité au Cœur du système douanier congolais", in *Revue des Douanes congolaises*, numéro spécial, septembre 2015, p. 15.

taxes on imported and exported goods. However, Excise mainly deals with taxation on local products and import excisable goods. Another major reform made in the Congolese modern customs was on the Excise domain as well. It means, although the Excise legislation was published in 2012 almost after the implementation of customs reform and modernization programme in 2003, it was included among the reform programme issues. The reason to get a new excise legislation was obvious. Established by the Order-law N068-010 of January 06, 1968, it became outdated. It means, it was no longer adapted to excise modern environment. So, within the framework of reform and modernization it was mandatory to elaborate a new Excise legislation which complies with the current management of Excise at the DRC directorate General of Customs and Excise.

The Excise Code[103] embodies the following innovations:

- the need of new technologies of information and communication in the management of producers of products subject to excise duty as well as in the formalities of declaration of the products of excise routed of their materialisation;
- the redefinition of the procedures and the formalities relating to the declaration of profession, the statement of work and the declaration of excise products, for better readability and transparency in operations;
- the simplification and streamlining of procedures and Excise controls, integration in the law from the basis of calculation of the oil taxation on imports, the introduction of measures against corruption;

[103] Carol Lutaladio Mbuta, Directeur Général Adjoint chargé des questions techniques, « Le nouveau code des Accises » in *Revue des douanes*, N°009, juin 2013, p17.

- the strengthening of penalties and the system to combat fraud by the redefinition of excise offences.

c) Connected legislations

Connected legislation means laws relating to prohibitions and restrictions. That is, necessary laws to fight against money laundering, counterfeiting and piracy, illicit trafficking in endangered species, illicit trafficking of cultural heritage, etc. Although there is no specific new code related to this legislation so far, this book deems that the Customs code embodies some provisions concerning these issues especially the section one, Articles 74 to 84 devoted to prohibitions and restrictions the DRC customs officers must apply while performing their job [104]. Eg. How to protect IPR.[105]

2. Single window or customs automation

As far as trade in goods is concerned, a single window can be considered as an environment where by different services evolving together agree that one of them perceive duties and rights on their behalf to facilitate the job.

Concerning international trade, a single window is considered as a cross border, intelligent, facility that allows parties involved in trade and transport to lodge standardised information, mainly electronic, with a single entry point to fulfill all import, export and transit related regulatory requirements.

A single window offers the following benefits for government: supply chain security increased, more effective and efficient use of resources, correct revenue

---

[104] Code des Douanes, 51ème Numéro spécial, *Journal Officiel de la République Démocratique du Congo*, Cabinet du Président de la République, 26 décembre 2010, pp.39-42.

[105] See also Non-tariff measures.

yields, improved trader compliance and increased accuracy of trade figures.

It also offers the industry the following advantages: reduced cost of compliance, faster clearance and release, predictable application/explanation of rules, effective and efficient deployment of resources[106].

In the DRC, the implementation of single windows in customs seems to be the most achieved measures of the customs reform and modernisation in this country in that customs revenues were highly increased. Aaron Cianyi Kayembe[107] provides the following statistics in congolese currency:104,03 billion in 2004, 145,57billion in 2005, 195,7 in 2006, 277,91 in 2007, 424,22 in 2008, 529,39 in 2009 and 754,51 billion in 2010. Globally, customs revenue increased around 33,48% per year with a peak of 52,65% in 2007 and 2008.

It should be noted, however, that within the framework of customs reform and modernisation, there were some single windows implemented in the DRC customs. Mention can be made of: Kin aero in 2000, Matadi in 2003, Kin-Est in 2007, and Kasumbalesa in 2010.

3. Tariff measures

a) Tariff

As said previously, the World Trade Organisation does not encourage taxes on export. The reason is, once the exported goods pay duties in the originating country, they will be sold very higher at the country of destination.

---

[106] Gareth Lewis, WCO customs data model; About Single Window, Munster 2008, pp 4-6

[107] Aaron Cianyi Kayembe, *Deo Rugwiza, une décennie d'un engagement basé sur la bonne gouvernance et l'éthique professionnelle*. Kinshasa, 2015, p.32.

Although the World Trade Organisation backs this principle, the country has its sovereignty. That is why, GATT Article 20 states that for reasons related to the protection of health, environment, public moral necessary to protect human, animal or plant life or health, gold or silver (…) the state can impose taxes but not higher ones[108]. One can say that this article gives the DRC customs the power to levy duties both on export and import.

In 2003, within the framework of customs reform and modernisation, by Law N° 002/ 03 of 13 March, 2003 establishing a new tariff for taxes and duties, a new tariff was promulgated[109].

The 2003 tariff like all the DRC previous customs tariffs comprises both export and import parts. Details on these issues are dealt with as follows:

i. Export tariff

By export products, we mean the movement of goods leaving originating countries abroad. As a geological scandal the economy of the DRC is mainly based on raw materials. That is why, for fiscal and economic reasons, the DRC levies export duties on some products.

It means that Export tariff, on the other hand, is based on the principle of non-taxation of goods. While certain specific products are taxed for economic policy and strategic reasons, the applied rate is fairly low, varying from one percent to ten per cent on an exhaustive list of seven products: green coffee; minerals and concentrates;

---

[108] World Trade Organisation, Trade Policy, DRC, 20 october 2010, p.52.

[109] Office des Douanes et Accises(OFIDA), Tarifs des Droits et Taxes à l'importation (Loi n°002/03 du 13mars 2003) article 1 et à l'exportation (Loi n°003/03 du 13mars 2003) article 1.

minerals oils; electric power; timber logs and square-edged sawn wood; fresh water; and metal scrap [110].

ii. Import tariff

Within the framework of the reform and modernisation programme, the customs tariff structure shifted from five rates to three ones including the zero tariff. These rates are: 5%, 10% and 20%. It means, the party nomenclature is full transposition of the 2002 version of the Harmonised System (H.S). It includes the new categorisation of products made by WCO and the creation, modification and deletion of certain tariff headings of H.S.[111].

iii. Tariff measures

This part is devoted to negotiations the DRC had with different partners or agreements signed with them.

So, the European Union is one of the DRC's major trading partners, in terms of both imports and exports of goods and services. Along with the other ECCAS countries, the DRC is participating in the negotiation of the Economic Partnership Agreement (EPA) between the ACP States and the European Union. The DRC benefits from the trade preferences of other developed countries in accordance with the national preference schemes, including the Generalized System of Preferences. The DRC has been eligible for the United States' African Growth and Opportunity Act (AGOA), Public Law 106 of 18 May since 2004[112].

---

[110] World Trade Organisation, Trade policy, review body, DRC, 11 may 2016, p.26

[111] For more details, read Mwange Muteba, *op.cit.*, p31-32.

[112] World Trade Organisation, Trade policy, review body, DRC, 11 may 2016, p.26

As previously said, in 2004, china signed a GSP regime with the least developing African countries, among them the DRC.[113]

b) Non tariff measures

Talking about these issues it is proper to argue that since the DRC has been a member of the WCO, WTO, etc., it has incorporated these organizations non-tariff measures into its customs regulations to comply with them and avoid conflicts while applying non-tariff measures on the ground. Hence, the WTO[114], quotes Article 13 of Special Law N°73-009 of 5 January 1973 on trade, as amended in 1974 which stipulates that the Minister responsible for foreign trade is empowered to take restrictive measures and prohibit the import of certain products. Such measures may be taken for reasons of security and morality, in order to protect public health and the environment, or because of their strategic nature. The exchange regulations define the list of products subject to prior declarations, the corresponding regime being administered by the Central Bank of the Congo. Frontier traffic is not affected. The goods subject to import and restrictions are, in principle, those indicated in the customs tariff and the exchange regulations. However, the World Customs Organisation CEN database states records Customs seizures and offences classified under 13 different product headings covering the main fields of customs enforcement activity[115]; That are: drugs, tobacco, beverage, CITES, Intellectual Property Rights, precursors, tax and duty evasion, weapons and explosives, currency, nuclear materials, hazardous materials, pornography/pedophilia and other prohibitions and

---

[113] cf. Chap 2.

[114] WTO, *op.cit.*, p.50.

[115] CEN WCO-OMD (Bookleaft).

restrictions . Medicines and human pharmaceutical and strategic products have been added to the list.

So, in total there are 15 products so far in the CEN database. We hope the list will be extended to other products in the future.

4. Valuation

In his notes, Achim Rogmann[116] defines Customs valuation as a procedure applied to determine the value of imported goods where customs duties are calculated in ad valorem terms.

We know two systems of value so far : the Brussels definition of customs valuation and the valuation according to GATT Article VII.

Let us consider each system.

a) Brussels definition of valuation

According to Brussels, customs valuation is a system for the valuation of imports for the application of ad valorem duties, adopted in 1953 following attempts to establish a European customs union[117]. Tthe Brussels definition of customs valuation should be the theoretical concept. It means, under the Brussels Customs Valuation, a normal price, i.e the usual competition price, was compared with the price negotiated by the trade partners. The price actually paid should be compared with this normal price and if necessary-adjusted in order to calculate the import duties. A normal price is the price that a good would fetch in an open market between a buyer and seller independent of each other, was determined for

---

[116] Achim Rogmann, *Customs valuation Law: The EU Model*, unpublished, 2008, p.3.

[117] http://lawin.org/Brussels- definition of value. Accessed on April 18, 2016.

each product, according to which the customs duty was ascertained.[118]

The Brussels valuation is the method which was used by the DRC customs administration until 2003. But with the customs reform and modernization programme this administration shifted from that valuation system to the WTO valuation one we are talking about in the following item.

b) Valuation according to General Agreement on Tariffs and Trade (GATT): article VII

The history of GATT 1994/WTO passes through Uruguay Round and Marrakech Agreements.

i. Background of Uruguay Round and Marrakech Agreements

In our Master thesis entitled Counterfeiting and Piracy in import and export; a strategy of the DRC[119], we argue, mankind has drawn experience from disastrous consequences and atrocities of wars on human life sectors, namely from the first and the second World Wars. Victimised by these wars, the same human being has been shaping different paths to avoid such disastrous situations in the future and improve his welfare. One of these paths is trade liberalisation through the Marrakesh agreement originating from Uruguay round with their ancestor's International Trade Organisation (ITO) and the General Agreement on Tariff and Trade (GATT).

After the economic crisis which occurred during and after the World War, two groups of different countries try

---

[118] Achim Rogmann, *op.cit.*, 2008, pp.4-5.

[119] Esamba Bokel, *Counterfeiting and Piracy in import and export; a strategy of the DRCongo* (Master Thesis), Munster University, Germany, 2008, pp. 26-27.

to sit together and find the way to solve the problem by creating the International Trade Organisation to regulate trade. Other countries also among which the United States of America, Canada, the United Kingdom and others started other negotiations about GATT to get the reduction of tariff. Due to the American congress refusal to ratify the treaty, the ITO failed to be implemented. Then, another group composed of the USA, Canada and others pursued negotiations until they produced the General Agreement on Tariff and Trade (GATT 1947) focusing mainly on trade in goods. GATT 1947 was an international treaty not an organization. It had an incomplete institutional framework. There was no secretariat but only some bodies. With the Single undertaking principle under GATT 1947 people could decide what obligation to sign. Members could decide which part to agree. Due to these weaknesses and for the sake of finding trade liberalisation agreement, negotiations started again until members reached the Marrakesh agreement which produced GATT 1994 or the World Trade Organisation (WTO).

The WTO has then become an institutional framework, i.e a full organisation. It has a Secretariat with different bodies and dispute settlement bodies. With the World Trade Organisation, the Single undertaking got a big advantage in that, if you are silent in a vote, you agree. All aspects of trade and goods are discussed. The World Trade Organisation produced a package composed of General Agreement on Tariff and Trade (GATT), General Agreement on Trade in Services (GATS) and General Agreement on Trade related to Aspects of Intellectual Property Rights (TRIPS). From that time to date, every WTO member has the obligation to respect the package requirements. Members have the obligation to implement TRIPS to protect Intellectual Property Rights (IPR), etc.

Briefly, the GATT history can be summarised as follows: the first step devoted to commodities and tariffs began from 1947. The second step from 1959 to1979 put emphasis on tariff reduction and the last one the Uruguay Round from 1986 to 1994 which produced GATT 1994 or WTO adding the following new areas; General Agreement on Trade in Services and General Agreement on Trade-Related Aspects of Intellectual Property Rights (TRIPS)[120]. It means, out of this round on April 15, 1994 in Marrakesh, Morocco the agreement established the General Agreement on Tariff and Trade (GATT)1994 known as World Trade Organization(WTO) was born. That is what Feng[121], states as the Marrakesh Agreement ratified according to national procedures and which entered into force in 1995 as an international instrument legally binding engaging the responsibility of states.

Any reader may ask himself: **what is trade facilitation**?

In our view, trade facilitation implies free movement of goods, capitals and services in commerce. The WTO defines **trade facilitation** as "the simplification and harmonization of international trade procedures"[122]. However, the UN/CEFAT defines it as "the simplification, standardization and harmonization of procedures and associated flows required to move goods from seller to buyer and to make payment OECD"[123].

---

120 World Trade Organisation, the legal texts, the results of the Uruguay round of multilateral trade negotiations, 1997, p 433.

121 Feng X., Regional trade policy course introduction to the WTO legal affairs office, WTO secretariat, Windhoek, 2006.

122 Andrew Grainger, *Trade Facilitation Consulting Ltd*, 2008, p.3

123 Andrew Grainger, *Trade Facilitation Consulting Ltd*, A lecturer in four parts, 2008, p.24.

- And why trade liberalisation? And each time members fail to reach an agreement on trade liberalization, why do medias talk more about the issue? Why do intellects make a lot of comments on that?

Anybody involved in the matter can give his answer to the questions asked above. However, in our opinion, the issue of the multilateral trade system as states the WTO basic legal texts, aims at raising standards of living, reciprocal and mutually advantages or arrangements. It means, what the WTO has been seeking is liberalisation of trade system via tariff reduction, market improvement or access. Once done, this free trade will have the following effects: competition among enterprises, industries, sectors and between members' states. As result, there will be welfare gaining effects, economics of scale, innovations, etc.

Briefly, the World Trade Organisation concern is man welfare through multilateral trade system. That is why, once negotiations on GATT fail, the world encounters such reactions.

As far as WTO is concerned, the following question needs to be discussed.

ii. The impact of GATT 1994 or WTO on the customs job

Some people may ask many questions about the job performed by both the World Trade Organisation and the World Customs Organisation. An attempt to explain to readers what is performed by the two organizations is the following. The WTO establishes the framework as customs should be designed with respect to customs code or legislation. The WTO has an influence on customs especially on customs union, free trade, etc. The World

Trade Organisation and the World Customs Organisation are good partners and work hand in hand. The WTO and the WCO are significant players in international trade. It is clear that WTO negotiates multi-lateral trade agreements whilst the WCO administrates global customs standards. Together, their complementary roles facilitate the global supply[124]. It means, the impact of the WTO on customs is obvious as said in the chapter devoted to basics of customs policy.

In our view, the liberalisation of trade as embodied in the RKC including the implementation of single window is based on WTO principles. The Agreement on Trade facilitation is with no doubt the job performed by the WTO. It takes its sources from GATT 1994 Articles V, VII and X.

Today, the calculation of valuation at different customs Member administrations is based on GATT article VII. It is the fruit of the WTO Policy.

As far as trade facilitation is concerned, let us consider the Bali package and trade facilitation as amended Marrakesh GATT/WTO Agreement.

iii. Bali package and trade facilitation as amended Marrakesh GATT/WTO Agreement

The part devoted to the WTO shows that after the Second World War, members sought different means to solve the economic crisis via different rounds or negotiations which produced GATT 1947. Since GATT could not grant access market to developing countries, it did not solve the agricultural problem and did not stress on the development of developing countries, Doha rounds started to tackle those issues. Unfortunately, it failed

[124] www.google.org. Accessed on 7 May, 2017.

because the United States and EU were not willing to give up their agricultural subsidies. India's demand that it should be allowed to extend its domestic agricultural subsidies indefinitely was met by opposition from the USA, while Cuba, Bolivia, Nicaragua, and Venezuela objected to the removal of a text relating to the USA embargo against Cuba[125]. Since Members could not agree, the Uruguay round started and produced GATT 1994 or the WTO with new areas which are General Agreement on Trade in Services (GATS) and General Agreement on Trade related to Aspects of Intellectual Property Rights (TRIPS).

Members continued to negotiate in Cancun, Hong Kong, Geneva, Nairobi, Paris to find a solution to the issues raised in Doha, but without finding any compromise. These talks happened with Pascal Lamy as the Director General of the WTO. But upon the arrival of Roberto Azevdo, new Director General of WTO, talks continued until Members concluded the first international multilateral agreement on trade facilitation solving their discrepancies raised in the previous rounds during the 9th Conference of the WTO in Bali, Indonesia, on 3-7 december 2016.[126].

- **Provisions of Bali package**

Due to the fact that the issues which were sources of discrepancies between developed and developing countries or among WTO Members were solved, the first multilateral agreement on trade facilitation has made of these issues the Bali package. In other words, agricultural subsidies, market access for developing countries,

---

[125] www.thebalance.com/what-is-the-doha-round-of-trade-talks-3306365. Accessed on April 28, 2017.

[126] https://www.wikipedia.org/wiki/Bali_package. Accessed on April 28,2017

reduction of import quotas for developing countries, trade facilitation which were the cause of failures of Doha, Cancun, Hong Kong and Geneva Conferences were taken into consideration in Bali since members agreed. These issues constitute what we call the "Bali package".

The Bali package mentioned above, covers the following four areas:

- Trade facilitation: simplify customs procedures to speed shipping.

- Development: grant developing countries greater access to developed markets.

- Food Security: temporarily allow poor countries to stockpile as much food as needed to get them through famines.

- Cotton: quotas on cotton imports (by developed countries) will be removed, along with deep subsidies (from emerging market countries).[127].

This leads us to the trade facilitation convention agreed hereafter:

- **WTO Agreement on Trade Facilitation**

Some readers may ask the reason why we consider the Bali package as the first multilateral agreement WTO members have concluded to facilitate trade meanwhile GATT, GATS, TRIPS exist. In our view, the GATT package although existing, problems relating to agriculture, subsidies, trade facilitation, market access were still arising since no consensus was reached on this issue.

Furthermore, considering TRIPS for example, the WTO imposes members to protect Intellectual Properties

---

[127] *Idem.*

Rights (IPR) but does not impose any template to follow. The WTO recommends members to adopt any policy they want to protect IPR. This is may be one of the reasons why, the WCO implemented a legislation model in 1998 to help members on this issue.

Concerning Trade Facilitation Agreement, as all members agree on issues which were sources of failure of the WTO previous negotiations, it is considered to be the first multilateral agreement. The Trade Facilitation Agreement (TFA) contains twelve articles regarding Trade Facilitation and Customs Cooperation in Section I, ten articles on special and differential treatment for developing countries and least-developed countries in Section II and two articles on institutional arrangements and final provisions in Section III[128].

Concerning the DRC position on trade facilitation convention, its government has started a ratification process which is underway.

After being through GATT and its outcomes, let us come back to the valuation according to GATT Article VII.

iv. An application of customs value according to GATT article VII

According to the Agreement on Implementation of Article VII of the General Agreement on Tariffs and Trade 1994, while calculating the goods value to levy customs duties, customs should consider the transaction value as defined in Article 1. Article 1 which is to be read together with Article 8, says, the customs value of imported goods shall be the transaction value, that is the price actually paid or payable for the goods when sold for export to the

[128] Ibidem.

country of importation adjusted in accordance with the provisions of Article 8. Article 8 stipulates, in determining the customs value under the provisions of Article1 that there shall be added to the price actually paid or payable for the imported goods[129]. The Agreement Article 8 gives more details on the subject.

Briefly, within the framework of implementation of Article VII of the GATT 1994, if the Article1 cannot help determine value, customs value shall use alternative valuation methods: transaction value of identical goods. If this does not march, the valuation method of similar goods shall be applied. In case it does not march, the deductive method should be applied. If the deductive method does not work, computed method and finally the fall-back method shall be applied. The Agreement stipulates that the methods quoted above shall be used in a hierarchical order but there is a reverse order between Articles 5 and 6. The Agreement of the WTO (GATT) gives more details on this issue.

v. The implementation of article VII in the DRC

As already said above, valuation was among issues embodied in the programme of reform and modernisation in 2003. To comply with the WTO on this issue, as a WTO Member since 18 March 2003, date of the enactment of Law No. 009/ 03 on the customs valuation of goods by the President of the Republic after its adoption by the Transitional Parliament, the DRC has been applying the WTO valuation agreement to calculate the imported goods values[130]. However, a long this book, the

---

129 WTO Agreement on implementation of Article VII of the General agreement on Tariffs and Trade, Article 1, 1994.

130 Loi n°009/03 du 18mars 2003 relative à l'évaluation en douane des marchandises par le Président de la République après son adoption par le Parlement.

importance of customs for the budget of the DRC as a developing country has been explained. Mention has also been made of different challenges facing any developing country customs especially the case of some irregularities observed during the process of customs clearance of goods such as: capacity building, valuation, fraud, corruption, etc. which have a negative impact on levying duties.

Since the DRC, as a developing country, needs fiscal revenue and different challenges mentioned above hamper customs to maximise customs and exices duties in an appropriate way, the company BIVAC has been authorised by the Government to carry out preshipment Inspection on behalf of the DRC since 1February 2006. Under the contract, Bivac inspection has to cover verification of the documents, quantity, price and tariff heading, on the one hand, and quality and conformity, on the other. Preshipment inspection applies to all imports irrespective of their mode of transport. It is carried out at the place of production, storage or shipment.[131].

5. Customs revue

Although published before the implementation of customs reform and modernisation programme, customs Revue seems to be the most visible medium of the DRC customs in that it contributed to the dissemination of this office activities to the audience during the reform period and to date.

6. Capacity building

Capacity building stands for different means used by any administration or service to fulfill its assigned objectives. Concerning customs staff training is among capacity building issues and draws any administration

[131] World Trade Organisation, Trade policy review, 11 May, p.38-39.

attention. To put that in other words, since 2005, the officers' training has retained the DGDA ruling committee attention in that many actions have been taken on capacity building. Mention can be made of: officers training at the Ecole Nationale des Finances, National School of Finances (ENF), Customs trainings in Kinshasa, North and South Kivu, Eastern Province, Bandundu, Maniema and the former Eastern Kasai,Trainings officers on Asycuda, in Kinshasa and Provinces, on customs code and other customs issues, Officers trainings at: the Cassablanca customs school in Morocco, the University of Munster in Germany, the Belgian customs school, the Customs school of Tourcoing in France and in South Africa, Switzerland, Mozambique, Zimbabwe, Burkina Faso, Japan, China and in South Korea[132].

A part from the actions discussed above, Social ones were also done.

C. COOPERATION WITH REGIONAL AND INTERNATIONAL ORGANISATIONS

According to Ricardo and Smith's theory, the liberalisation of economy triggers the population welfare, economic development, etc.Today, China seems to confirm the theory for the simple reason that contrary to the Mao era whereby China was in autarky, China has become the second world economy because it is opened to the world. It means, Ricardo and Smith's theory may be an incentive for nations to sign multilateral and bilateral agreements to belong to different regional and international organisations. However, due to difficulties

---

[132] Idelphonse Mubibya Silutala, "De l'Ofida à la DGDA: le long parcours vers le succès", *Revue des Douanes Congolaises* 2005-2015:10 ans de reformes et performances, numéro spécial, septembre 2015, pp.82-83.

nations face to implement multilateral agreements the WTO advises them to create Customs Union as stated in GATT article XXIV which stipulates that the contracting parties must recognize the desirability of increasing freedom of trade by the development, through voluntary agreements, of closer integration between the economies of the countries parties to such agreements. They must also recognize that the purpose of a customs union or of a free-trade area should be to facilitate trade between the constituent territories and not to raise barriers to trade of other contracting parties with such territories[133]. It should be noted, however, that customs union is a regional grouping where by different states have unified their trade in goods policies for the population welfare and reach development. Customs Union means: "a single customs territory, elimination of duties and other restrictions for substantially all trade originating in the territories of the union, a common customs tariff and common non-tariff barriers in trade with other territories"[134]. The regional integration or the formation of customs union or economic integration has the following steps: Free Trade, Customs Union, Economic Union and Monetary[135].

This seems to be the reason why, the DRC has become member of: SADC, COMESA, ECCAS, ECGLC at the regional level and also the WCO, WTO and UN member at the international level.

Let us talk briefly about the DRC belonging to each organisation:

---

[133] World Trade Organisation, *the results of the Uruguay round of multilateral trade negotiations*, 1997, p. 458

[134] Michael Lux, Head of Unit, GATTXXIV Taxud/c/4 the formation of Customs union, p.8.

[135] Wieslaw Czyzowicz, Customs Policy Module-Legal and Practical Approach (Master of Customs Administration Course), University of Muenster, Germany, May,15-16, 2008, p. 12.

I. Regional level

1. The DRC customs and ECGLC (CEPGL)

ECGLC is the Economic Community of the Great Lakes Countries. It is a sub-regional organisation with multiple vocation created by the signing of the Agreement of Gisenyi in Rwanda on September 20, 1976, aiming at insuring the safety of member states, at favoring the creation and the development of activities of public interest, at promoting the trades and the traffic of the persons and the possessions, at establishing the cooperation in a narrow way in all the domains of the political, economic and social life.[136]

It comprises three members states which are: Burundi, Democratic Republic of the Congo and Rwanda. Its purpose is to promote regional economic cooperation and integration. The DRC became member on 13 June, 1978.

The ECGLC has some institutions under its controls: Bank of Development of the States of the Great Lakes (BDEGL), the Economic Community of the Great Lakes Countries Organization for Energy (EGL), etc.[137]

2. The DRC customs and SADC

It is known worldwide that after the slavery which took place between the 15th and the 19th centuries, African countries remained under the colonization. If some of them such as the DRC in Central Africa got its independence around 1960, it was not the case with Southern African countries. For example, South Africa, was ruled by the minority of white men under the

---

[136] http://en.wikipedia.org/wiki/economic_community_of_the_great_lake_country. Accessed on 04 June, 2016.

[137] http://en.wikipedia.org/wiki/economic_community_of_the_great_lake_country. Accessed on 04 June, 2016.

Apartheid regime. Formerly, Southern Rhodesia, Zimbabwe was under the British colonization. That is why, to fight against apartheid, Southern African countries decided to join their efforts via diplomacy, politics and military. This, led to the birth of Southern Africa Development Co-ordination Conference (SADCC).[138].It means that, even if SADCC had pursued different objectives, but the major one was to get freedom from the white man oppression in their homeland especially in South Africa where Apartheid became bitter. In 1990, the South Africa President Frederick De Klerk took two important decisions. The first decision was to remove the ban on the ANC (African National Congress led by Nelson Mandela who spent 27years in prison to claim for equality between black and white people) and several other anti-apartheid organizations. The second one was the release of Nelson Mandela on February 11, 1990 after 27 years, 6 months and 6 days of imprisonment.[139] It was the collapse or the end of apartheid in South Africa.

In other words, the release of Nelson Mandela led to the abolition of Apartheid and the arrival of democracy in South Africa especially with his election as the first black President in 1994. This situation had an impact on the Southern African region policy.

In 1992, the SADCC shifted into SADC (Southern African Development Community)[140]. Like SADCC, SADC pursues many objectives but the main one is the regional integration for the welfare of the community citizens. The following states are members of SADC: Botswana, Angola, Lesotho, Democratic Republic of Congo, Malawi, Madagascar, Mauritius, Comores,

---

[138] en.wikipedia.org/wiki/southern_African_Development_community .Accessed on 04 june, 2016

[139] https://www.sadc.int/member-states. Accessed on 08 June, 2016

[140] Ibidem.

Mozambique, Namibia, Seychelles, Swaziland, South Africa, Tanzania, Zimbabwe and Zambia. The DRC has become member of SADC since 1996 with the arrival of Alliance of Democratic Forces for the Liberation of Congo in French, Alliance des Forces Démocratiques pour la libération du Congo (AFDL) led by Laurent Desiré Kabila.

Concerning SADC, Out of 16 members Angola, Malawi, the DRC and Seychelles have not yet acceded to the FTA since its launch in 2008. In addition to the FTA, there are provided for the establishment of a Customs Union in 2010, the operationalization of common market in 2015 and the use of a single currency by 2018. Progress has been made within this community in the implementation of the FTA, particularly the revision of rules of origin, the removal of barriers or non-tariff barriers. For better implementation of its integration programme, SADC has established a Regional Indicative Strategic Development Plan (DPRIS) that aligns with the Millennium Development Goals and covers the areas of industrialization, economic and social issues.[141].

3. The DRC customs and COMESA

In traditional African culture people used to live in extended families whereby you find the father, mother, children, their brothers, sisters, cousins, etc. living together. In spite of the impact of colonisation (Western culture) on the African tradition, living in a community is purely African.

Yet, we know that the creation of customs union complies with the World Trade Organisation, Article XXIV. In a broader sense, it complies also with African culture in that both in customs union and African culture,

---

[141] www.sadc.org. Accessed on 04 June, 2016.

people think, they are together, they belong to the same country, it exists team buildings. That is, people work together, etc.

Concerning SADC, it has been created after COMESA, but it seems to be mainly composed of Southern African English speaking countries a part from the Democratic Republic of Congo, Mozambique, Angola, Madagascar, Mauritius and Seychelles although some of them were or are still members of COMESA. What is COMESA? It is the Common Market for Eastern and Southern Africa. COMESA was formed in December 1994, replacing a Preferential Trade Area which had existed since 1981.

In 2008, COMESA agreed to an expanded free-trade zone including members of two other African trade blocs, the East African Community (EAC) and the Southern Africa Development Community (SADC). [142]. The following are Members states of Comesa: Comores, Democratic Republic of Congo, Angola, Djibouti, Burundi, Egypt, Ethiopia, Erythrea, Kenya, Mauritius, Madagascar, Malawi, Uganda, Rwanda, Seyschelles, Sudan, Zambia, Swaziland and Tanzania. The DRCongo joined it on 21 december 1981 since Preferential Trade Area[143].

Kiesse argues that four members including the DRC are finalising the process of membership of COMESA. For the DRC, a tariff reduction is scheduled over three years, a calling process a gradual liberalisation of rights (tariff), at the rate of a reduction of 40% of tariffs in the first year, 30% the second year and 30 others the third year.

---

[142] Maximilien Kiese –a-Ngunda, « A travers la DGDA, la RDC en plein dans les communautés économiques régionales », in *2005-2015 :10 ans de reformes et performances, Revue des Douanes Congolaises* , numéro spécial, septembre 2015,pp.43-44

[143] https://en.wikipedia.org/wiki/common _market_for_Eastern _and_Southern_Africa. Accessed on 17 june, 2016.

The effectiveness of this reduction of rights must be taken into account in the rate of duties and taxes for imports through legislation, of which the application will include two rates of the customs duties, one reserved to the Member States of COMESA and other non-members .At the end of these three years of gradual liberalisation, the COMESA products will be subject to zero percent of the customs duties thus embodying the membership of the DRC to the free trade area.[144]. It should be noted that EAC, COMESA and SADC have started negotiations for unification.

4. The DRC customs and Economic Community of Central African States (ECCAS)

The ECCAS[145] is an Economic Community of the African Union for promotion of regional economic co-operation in Central Africa. It aims at achieving collective autonomy, raising the standard of living of its populations and maintain economic stability through harmonious. The Economic Community of Central African States was created by the Treaty of Libreville in 1983[146].

The ECCAS members states are: Cameroon, Burundi, Central African Republic, Chad, Equatorial Guinea, Gabon, Sao Tome and Principe, the Republic of Congo and the Democratic Republic of Congo which became member on 18 October 1983[147].

As can be seen through its date of creation, the ECCAS had been existing before COMESA and SADC and had outlined its integration stages. But, due to economic

---

[144] Ibidem. Accessed on 04 June,2016

[145] In French: Communauté Économique des États de l'Afrique Centrale, CEEAC.

[146] Maximilien Kiese –a-Ngunda, op.cit.

[147] https://en.wikipedia.org/wiki/Economic_community_of_central_African_state.Accessed on 17 june, 2016.

problems and wars which occurred in some of its members states such as Burundi, Central African Republic, Congo, the DRC, this community has not yet been able to implement its integration policy. However, COMESA AND SADC have taken a step forward since both of them have started implementing their integration stages step by step.

It should be noted, however, that the lack of this integration programme implementation has become also the community concern.[148]

II. International level

1. DRC customs and the World Customs Organisation

The World Customs Organisation evolved from a study Group formed to examine customs issues identified by the GATT. It has been created in 1948, first as the Customs Committee of what was post World War 2 Committee for European Economic Co-operation. In 1952 the committee evolved into the Customs Co-operation Council (with 17 founding members-all Europeans). In 1994, to recognize its wordwide growth, it adopted the name World Customs Organization (WCO) [149]. But its official name remains Customs Co-operation Council.

The World Customs Organization has 182 members states, today. Aaron Cianyi Kayembe states that the DRC has become member of the WCO since July 26th, 1972.[150].

The World Customs Organization has been created to secure the highest degree of harmony and uniformity

---

[148] Ibidem.

[149] World Customs Organization, Diary 2018 p.11. see also www.google.com. Accessed on 07 May, 2018.

[150] Aaron Cianyi Kayembe, *op.cit.*, 2015.pp. 32-33.

customs systems and especially to study the problems inherent in the development and improvement of customs technique and customs legislation, in the interest of international trade to promote co-operation between Governments in these matters, bearing in mind the economic and technical factors involved therein. It is an independent intergovernmental body whose mission is to enhance the effectiveness and efficiency of Customs administrations.[151]

Accordingly, it is a competent worldwide organisation in customs expertise which plays an important role in developing and responding to the needs of members in customs matters. As shown through its objective and definition, the WCO is an international organization of reference in terms of customs since it provides affiliated members with different instruments and tools such as:

a- The Revised Kyoto Convention (RKC)

A long this book, we have quoted the Revised Kyoto convention many times.

First of all, there was the Kyoto Convention which was adopted as the international convention on simplification and harmonisation of customs procedures on 19 May, 1973 and entered into force in 1974[152]. However, due to the fact that the way it was structured was not good to apply a high level of harmonisation, its revision became mandatory. Then, the Revised Kyoto Convention was produced and entered into force in February 2006. It is

---

[151] http://www.wcoomd.org/en/about-us/what-is-the-wco.aspx. accessed on 4 June, 2016.
[152]. World Customs Organization, *Compliance and facilitation directorate, facilitation and procedures sub-directorate*, p.2.

considered like a blueprint for simple and efficient customs procedures for the 21st century[153].

It means, although some of its weaknesses which require its revision again, the Revised Kyoto Convention is considered as the model in terms of facilitation and simplification of customs procedures to date. It shows customs different paths to reform and modernise their administrations. That is why, it is perceived as a key in framework of standards in the reforms of all customs legislations today. A lot of administrations such as the Democratic Republic of Congo have reformed their customs code referencing to it although its non-ratification by this country. The RKC recommends customs to use Risk management to have balance between control and facilitation. To enhance customs control, it recommends that customs should seek cooperation and conclude mutual assistance agreements with other customs administrations and memoranda of understanding with the private sector. The RKC recommends customs to use information technology to have exchange of information between customs administrations. It requires the use of computerisation to do good risk analysis and the implementation of single window for good border management, especially the cooperation between customs and other agencies evolved at borders, etc.[154]

b- Istambul Convention

Istambul Convention is a single instrument for simplification and harmonisation of temporary admission

---

[153] World Customs Organization, the Revised Kyoto Convention, General Annex guidelines, 2000, p.2.
[154] *Ibidem*, p.25.

formalities signed in 1990. It has replaced all conventions dealing solely or principally with temporary admission[155].

c- Harmonised System (HS)

In 1991, the WCO launched an initiative to improve classification of goods in customs especially problems encountered by developing countries on this issue. Some missions of diagnosis were sent to different countries. The purpose was to see procedural problems in classifying goods in developing countries, since a good and uniform classification of goods facilitates trade and investment, promote compliance with trade laws and reduces losses of revenue. After these missions, the WCO produced a good classification model recommendation in 1998.[156]

d- Framework of standards Safe (FOS)

As mentioned above, the role of customs in the 21st century is security and nobody ignores the influence of Western on different sectors of human life: politics, economy, religion, etc., especially the America in modern society. It seems that due to the 11 September, 2001 attacks which took place in the World Trade Center in America, that security has become a new paradigm in customs mainly the security of supply chain. The focus of Customs in many countries has moved from import control to export one. Eg: China, Singapore, Australia.

The terrorist attacks in America seem to be one of the reasons why, the WCO has implemented the Framework of Standards SAFE (FOS) in 2006 to secure the supply chain.

In short, This FOS started with two pillars which are cooperation between customs to customs and cooperation

---

155 World Customs Organisation, Istanbul Convention, p.3.
156 World Customs Organisation, Convention on Harmonised System.

between customs and private sector. Another pillar, cooperation between customs and different agencies especially at border has been added.

- ***Cooperation between customs-to-customs:***

It includes: integrated supply chain management, technology, risk management, advance information, integrity, security assessments, customs co-operation[157].

As said in the RKC part, the FOS 1st pillar is needful since it allows an efficient customs control in both import and export[158]. While performing the job at the RILO Central Africa, experience has shown that to have sufficient information related to CITES products for example from our region seized in Asia Pacific, cooperation between Central Africa and Asia Pacific customs administrations via the Regional Intelligence Liaison Offices for Central Africa (RILO –CA) and Regional Intelligence Liaison Office for Asia Pacific (RILO AP) was the unique means of communication.

- ***Cooperation between Customs-to-Business***

It comprises: partnership, security, authorisation, technology, communication and facilitation[159].

To start with, let us compare this pillar to tradition and modern pedagogies. In ancient pedagogy, the teacher was the center of education in that he was doing everything without considering any pupils' consent. As a dictator, pupils were obliged to obey everything whether good or not.

---

[157] World Customs Organisation, Data Model, 2006, p.16.

[158] *Idem.*

[159] *Idem.*

That is why, pupils sometimes learnt by heart some lessons without really understanding that. Despite of its weaknesses, former pedagogy had a lot of achievements especially in the DRC where people consider that the education got in the former time was better than the one pupils get nowadays undermined by a lot of irregularities.

In our opinion, it is understandable that the former education was better than nowadays education since people in the former times had good livings conditions. But, due to the fact the ancient pedagogy did not consider the pupil as the center of education, modern pedagogues, after different experimentations, have reached the conclusion that the pupil is the cornerstone or the center of his education. Therefore, all education must take into account his needs. The pupil should get education which relates to his capacities, level and interests. Education based on pupil's needs will achieve expected results. It is even the foundation of the modern pedagogy why not of modern child psychology.

The issue of former and modern pedagogies mentioned above, relates to the second pillar of framework of standard while talking about non complier customs management and customs complier management in that in non-complier management, customs was doing everything without any agreement or dialogue with the business sector. However, laws applied by customs in this way had a negative impact on the business sector.

Like the modern pedagogy, the FOS second pillar has understood the issue and claims for cooperation with business sector via the consultative process implemented by the WTO. Although it is difficult, it is necessary in customs because implemented measures are costly for business sector and need to ask them money. Through dialogue it is possible to convince the private sector by giving them some privileges while fulfilling their customs formalities or jobs.

Here, the notion of Agreed Economic Operator (AEO) becomes very important since through the implementation of AEO, you can convince the private sector that they will get facilitation, security, etc while doing their business with customs.

- ***Cooperation between customs and other agencies***

Our experience as customs officer in developing countries shows that while performing our job on the ground, conflicts sometimes arise between customs and other agencies when it is the question to share per-diem after a service rendered or advantages related to any service. Since other agencies believe that customs get more privileges than them, cooperation with these services becomes obligatory. Cooperation via the single window is beneficial since any service gets the fruit of its service rendered. As result, this helps exchange of information, good collaboration, enhance cooperation to combat fraud and avoid corruption since all services feel working in a team.

e- Arusha Declaration

Globally, customs officers are perceived like corrupted people working to the detriment of their government public purse. It means, considered to be corrupted, customs officers are also triggers of fraud. To solve the problem, WCO members signed the Arusha declaration which aims at helping customs officers to combat corruption in their job. It focuses even on the issuance of code of conduct for them on this endeavour.

f- Strategic Trade Control (STCE) implementation guide

As said in chapter 3, within the framework of its Security Programme, the WCO has produced the Strategic Trade Control Enforcement (STCE) implementation Guide which responds to requests from the World Customs Organization (WCO) members for practical assistance related to enforcing strategic trade controls. It should serve as a guide for WCO members in the development and review of their Strategic Trade Control Enforcement (STCE).[160].

g- Mutual Administrative Assistance(MAA)

There is a Ndengese saying, "Bovo bomoko apaketaka basa bamfulu bape". It means, one hand cannot handle two bird kids. To be clear, a person or a company cannot be self-sufficient; they need other people. This saying relates to customs in its fight against fraud in that customs needs cooperation with other customs to succeed on this issue. It is the reason why, in 2003, the WCO produced the Mutual Administrative Assistance to provide administration members each other with assistance to the prevention, investigation and combating of customs offenses and to ensure the security of the international trade supply chain[161].

h- Customs Enforcement Network (CEN)

The WCO has implemented the **Customs Enforcement Network (CEN)** with its applications. They are CEN which is a database of customs seizures and offences, comprising non-nominal data required for

---

[160] World Customs Organisation, Strategic Trade Control enforcement (STCE), Implementation guide, p.7.

[161] WCO, Mutual Administrative Assistance, Article 2.

analysis of the illicit traffic in the various areas of customs' competence, the **Customs Enforcement Network Communication (CENcomm)** platform conceived as a web-based system permitting a closed user group to exchange messages via encrypted channels, in real time,24-hours-a-day for the duration of an operation or project and **national Customs Enforcement Network(nCEN)**, a system developed by WCO to assist Customs administrations with the collection and storage of law-enforcement information at the national level, with the additional capability to exchange this information at regional and international level.[162]. A part from these applications, there is also the CEN web site containing various enforcement related to analtytical reports, publications and alerts. Accordingly, **CEN** is an international database which embodies seizures and customs offences for the sake of intelligence. Those data are non-nominal. **CENcomm** is a secured tool or platform for communication during a project or operation. Eg. goalkeeper operation related to the fight against counterfeit and pirated goods of football equipment of the world cup 2018 in Russia, environet platform (project) dedicated to communictaion on seizures, information related to CITES products. However, **nCEN** is a national data base which comprises seizures and offences related to fraud.

Accordingly, **CEN** and **nCEN** have both similarities and differences. Their similarities lie on the fact that they are databases, they comprise seizures and offences for intelligence purposes.

However, their differences lie on that **CEN** is an international database, while **nCEN** is a national one.

[162] WCO, leaflet sharing connecting and bridging.

CEN database comprises non-nominal, but nCEN embodies nominal data.

A part from the CEN, the WCO has implementd an Information and Intelligence Centre (I2C) at its HQ to facilitate communication and coordination on Customs compliance and law enforcement-related matters.[163]

i- Interface Public Member (IPM)

Interface Public Member has been created to allow front line officers to combat counterfeiting and piracy while performing their job on the ground. IPM allows the identification of genuine and fake goods.

It should be noted, however, that a part from these tools mentioned above, the WCO has implemented other instruments and tools in valuation, for example, a customs valuation compendium although not binding for customs administrations, but can inspire some members. In spite of the failure to sign an accepted convention on rules of origin, there is a guide for technical update of preferential rules of Origin. The Columbus programme for capacity building at different administrations has been implemented.

At the regional level, the WCO has created some regional entities such as eleven Regional Intelligence Liaison Offices (RILOs) at its six regions for collecting and analysing data as well as disseminating information on trends, mode operandi, routes and significant cases of fraud.[164].That is, to fight fraud related to illicit trafficking and disseminates information via mutual administrative among different members. The network works with the Customs Enforcement Network (CEN) and comprises 3 stakeholders. The WCO Secretariat at the international

---

[163] www.wcoomd.org. Accessed on 02 June, 2018.
[164] *Idem.*

level, the Regional Intelligence Liaison Office at the regional level and the National Contact Point at the National one. This network is known as the Global Regional Intelligence Network (GRN). WCO has also created the Regional Offices for capacity Building (ROCBs) to follow up the process of reform and modernisation in customs administrations, the Regional Training Centers (RTCs) to provide different trainings to its members; the Regional Customs Laboratories to train members for identification of chemicals and analysing chemicals samples for HS classification and trade control; and the Regional Dog Training Centers (RDTCs) to fight against illicit trade using dogs on this issue.[165]. The list of WCO tools and instrument is not exhaustive.

2. DRC customs and World Trade Organisation (WTO)

Let us go before all through trade in ancient times. As argued in the first chapter, each geographical region got his way of dealing with commerce. Concerning trade in goods in traditional Africa in the Democratic Republic of Congo especially at the Dekese territory, it was mainly based on exchange of goods by means of cowrie (Isangi in Ndengese language) as stated Bamba. Coming back to Asakura, it is very difficult to state the period customs started exactly. However, some written texts such as Portorium for Romans, the fact diplomats were 78 already exempted from customs duties, the doctrine of Colbert in France, the export of copper and metal in Katanga before colonisation mentioned in the first chapter, show how customs started a long time ago although it was not named customs officially.

---

[165] World Customs Organisation, Diary 2018, pp 35-37.

Coming back to Ancient Africa, characterised by oral tradition as source of information, it was difficult to state from which period trade in goods had existed. Furthermore, principles governing this source of information sometimes embodied in proverbs, tales, etc were really kept by a group of people mainly old ones transmitting them from generation to generation. That is why, paraphrasing Amadou Hampâté Bâ, the death of an old man equals the loss of the library. It means being considered as reference or wise person in society, whenever an old man passes away, there is a gap in the society concerned. Due to the fact that oral tradition embodies some weaknesses especially the lack of archives, distortion of information through rumours phenomenon causing sometimes violence, misunderstanding, etc, the written source has been perceived as an excellent means of communicating or implementing legislation related to any domain via documents. It allows for example the signatory of agreements stakeholders must comply with, while dealing with trade. It is the case with the WTO including its bindings laws related to trade facilitation and dispute settlements to solve conflicts in case stakeholders cannot reach agreements. That is why, this multilateral system of trade has become an international law to regulate international trade among affiliated mcmbers.

WTO has been presented deeply in the part devoted to GATT. So, no need for coming again to all the issue.

In short, it has officially come into existence the 1st January 1995 under the Marrakesh Agreement, signed by 123 nations on 15 April 1994, replacing the General Agreement on Tariffs and Trade (GATT), which commenced in 1948. The WTO deals with regulation of trade between participating countries by providing a framework for negotiating trade agreements and a dispute resolution process aimed at enforcing participants' adherence to WTO agreements, which are signed by representatives of member governments and ratified by their parliaments. The DRC has become its member since January 1, 1997[166].

3. DRC Customs and United Nations

The name "United Nations", coined by United States President Franklin D. Roosevelt was first used in the Declaration by United Nations of 1 January 1942, during the Second World War, when representatives of 26 nations pledged their Governments to continue fighting together against the Axis Powers. The United Nations officially came into existence on 24 October 1945.[167]

As states its name, the United Nations is an international organisation which gathers several governments or states. It has a charter which gives him power to solve problems facing humanity via negotiations, dialogue and agreements. Those problems are: climate change, peace and security, sustainable development, human rights, disarmament, terrorism, humanitarian and health emergencies, gender equality, governance, food production, etc[168].

As a powerful organisation with binding obligations its charter gives the UN the power to take resolutions and impose sanctions, embargoes, etc. whenever members do not comply with or in some cases to keep a dangerous situation from occurring in a given state. It is the case with the Resolution 1540 to be applied by States customs administrations since it is difficult for the UN to

---

166 https://en.wikipedia.org/wiki/world_trade_organisation. Accessed on June 12.2016.

167 http://www.un.org/en/sections/history/history-united-nations/. Accessed on 4th May 2018.

168 *Idem.*

implement security measures at borders without customs. The DRC has become a UN member since 20 September, 1960.[169]

After going through all organisations especially regional ones, an important question we can ask is, although the WTO encourages members to create Customs Unions, the DRC belongs to multiple organisations. Is this the DRC multi belonging SADC, COMESA, CEPGL and ECCAS, a solution for its regional integration? This question is another topic of research we developed in Picard programme 2013.

This book will not go through it deeply but for the sake of information, the conclusion we reached concerning the issue is, the solution for the DRC is to belong to one Customs Union and to one FTA since once a member of different regional organisations a conflict can raise while applying laws (legislation, tariff) for each organisation. For details, see Jean-paul Esamba Bokel'Ipoka, Multibelonging, SADC, COMESA and ECCAS, a solution for the regional integration of the DRC in Picard Programme 2013.

---

[169] *Idem.*

CHAPTER 5

THE FUTURE OF CUSTOMS POLICY OF THE DRC

This chapter deals with the prospective customs policy of the DRC. It suggests also what is to be done after the implementation of the 2003 or any fourth coming programme of customs reform and modernisation in the DRC customs.

A. DETERMINANTS OF FUTURE CUSTOMS POLICY

A determinant can be defined as a factor which decides whether or how something happens. Noêl Copin[170] considers four determinants of customs policy future. They are: integration of the non-revenue tasks in security context, from physical checks at one point towards certification of the whole supply chain, from executor to coordinator of the data and checks on goods having a third country as place of origin or destination and change from paper era to digital one.

Let us go through each determinant.

I. Integration of the non-revenue tasks in security context

While performing their job, customs officers in developing countries pay mainly attention to customs

[170] Czysowich, *op.cit.*, 2008, p.18-26.

duties which are still the priority of the government and the most important source of the State's budget[171]. Integration of the non-revenue tasks in security context implies that matters relating to health and consumer protection, food safety and environmental risks, risks with respects to public security, illicit trade in weapons, drugs, cites, counterfeiting and piracy, currency, cultural heritage, fight against crime and terrorism[172] are very important in customs job and should deserve a particular attention. So, internal integration with different partners such as police, immigration, quarantine, economic affairs and others would be very crucial to fight these risks.

Concerning the DRC, as a developing country, although the fact that the fiscal role is the government priority, while performing their job customs officers in this country must consider the revenue collection as routine since it is the primary role of customs existing for ages they have made of an habit by focusing for example on tariff misclassification, valuation, exemption fraud. Now, Congolese officers have to stress much on risks mentioned above for their job security.

II. From physical checks at one point towards certification of the whole supply chain

While speaking about certification, what comes first in mind is an official document granted to someone who passed an exam, attended a conference, a seminar or a professional training, etc. There are different definitions of certification. In our context, Certification can be a useful tool to add credibility, by demonstrating that your product

---

[171] Michael Lux, *Guide to Community Customs Legislation*, Bruylant, 2002, p. 2.

[172] Noel Copin cited by Czyzowicz in Customs Policy Module-Challenges and Future (Master of Customs Administration Course), University of Muenster, Germany, May, 15-16, 2007, pp. 18-28.

or service meets the expectations of your customers. For some industries, certification is a legal or contractual requirement, the provision by an independent body of written assurance (a certificate) that the product, service or system in question meets specific requirements.

In customs, certification is very important since it is the basis for an efficient partnership. It allows duty compliance guarantee, compliance guarantees with respect to economic measures, security guarantee for the whole supply chain from manufacturer to consumer, facilitation of customs procedures, easier collection of data, etc.[173]

III. From executor to coordinator of the data and checks on goods having a third country as place of origin or destination executor

The issue of executor and coordinator shows the role of customs in supply chain. It is proper to argue that from the producer to the consumer, goods pass trough borders and Customs plays the Gatekeeper role or single contact point. It means, in case of automation for example, customs plays the coordinator role and cooperates with services in borders, to facilitate trade.

Concerning the issue of third country we deem that the creation of customs union, agreed regional economic operators (AEO) are mandatory since they are appropriate for that. They facilitate the supply chain in that members rely on each other on different mechanisms (certification for example) put in place and only goods going or coming from a third country can be checked.

IV. Digital era

To start with, the site www.igi-global.com, accessed on 4thJune, 2017, states, it is not easy to explain what we

[173] Noel Copin, op.cit., pp.22.

mean by digital era. That is, there are many useful ways of describing and discussing it. The Digital era is characterised by technology which increases the speed and breath of knowledge turnover within the economy and society. It can be seen as the development of an evolutionary system in which knowledge turnover is not only very high, but also increasingly out of control of humans, making it a time in which our lives become more difficult to manage. For example, in the second generation internet, 'the semantic web', functionality, which understands meaning, replaces the search function of unknowingly matching words, which often have multiple meanings. In time, within this version of the internet, software agents will exchange knowledge without human intervention. Concerning customs, it is well known that the WCO dedicated the 2016 year to Digital customs. The term Digital Customs refers to any automated or electronic activity that contributes to the effectiveness, efficiency, and coordination of customs activities, such as automated customs clearance systems, the single window concept, electronic exchange of information, websites to communicate information and promote transparency, and the use of smart phones.

In short, Digital era is the use of Information and Communication Technology (ICT) in any domain. Here, the emphasis is much placed on change from paper era to adopt automation or use of computer in customs which has the following advantages; visibility, transparency, accessibility of data, speedy processing, improvement of job, reliability, etc.

That is why, although digital era embodies internet as well, for the sake of visibility the use of internet is considered as an additional determinant as it is further presented.

In customs area, paperless is important to secure and facilitate international trade, prenotification on departure and on arrival offers the opportunity to assess risks, single window allows exchange of data on possible risks and integration of checks, paperless customs allows to lay the emphasis on export instead of import; allows the change of results of checks and risk analyses between Customs administrations in the framework of partnership; allows Customs formalities to be integrated with trade[174].

V. Additional determinants

In our view, a part from determinants mentioned above, DRC customs has additional ones which are: continuing growth of international trade, tariff will continue, levying duties on excisable goods, focusing the use of internet.[175]

- **Continuing growth of international trade**: the workload of the customs administration is largely driven simply by the magnitude of the trade flows with which it must cope.[176]

Due to its presence in borders, customs will always remain an important tool to back the growth of international trade.

-Tariff will remain an important source of revenue: Some people believe that trade liberalisation implies zero tariffs. However, Achim Rogmann[177] sustains that a central purpose of the GATT is to reduce and bind tariffs in that tariffs bind add security and predictability to GATT/WTO system. It means that although there has

---

[174] Noel Copin, op.cit., p.22.

[175] Michael Keen, *changing customs; Challenges and Strategies for the Reform of Customs Administration*, International Monetary Fund, October 20, 2003, p.5.

[176] Ibidem.

[177] Achim Rogmann, *Op.cit.*, 2008, pp.6-8.

been significant liberalization of trade over recent decades, in many countries trade tax rates continue to be quite high, and the receipts they yield are a key component of the public finances[178]. In other words, in spite of trade liberalisation, the WTO law is governed by the principle of tariffication. Market access provisions of the Uruguay Round Agreement require the immediate conversion (tariffication) of nontariff import barriers (such as quotas, restrictive licensing and variable levies) into tariff equivalents. In the future, countries will not be able to use nontariff measures to restrict trade. For the foreseeable future, in any event, the central lesson is clear: for many developing countries, and especially the poorest of them, tariff will continue to be a core component of government finances for many years to come[179].

- **Levying duties on excisable goods**: with trade liberalisation excise duties which depend on infant industries and excisable goods will be crucial and are considered to be the future of any customs administration. It is the case with the DRC which has a lot of raw materials to build such industries and focus on excise duties.

- **Focusing the use of internet**: Nowadays, internet is a crucial tool in customs since it is an open source in intelligence. Officers are requested to use it while producing intelligence cycle. That is, collection, evaluation, compilation, analysis and processing information. Paraphrasing Mikuriya, the Secretary General of the WCO's speech during the 36th Enforcement Committee session, today, people speak about internet of objects with visible effects on customs. The main concern for customs is, how to get data? There

---

[178] *Ibidem*, p.5.
[179] *Idem*

are many sources of data among which open ones but how to analyze data collected, what to do after analysis and how to share the fruits of data with different partners? This is the main concern of customs.

- **Future missions of the DRC customs:** accordingly, the use of customs determinants does not necessarily modify customs missions since customs should be at borders so long as the trade exists. However, new determinants mean, we have to use new control methods, techniques (…) while performing our job. We have to change the way of doing things to face new challenges.

So, the DRC customs missions are the same. They are: fiscal, economical, social, trade facilitation, external statistics and security.

After being through new determinants and customs missions, an important question we can ask is the following; are the DRC officers ready to apply new determinants and missions?

Before answering this important question, let us see what Czysowich said about the general situation in developing countries in the following item since the DRC is among them.

B. DEVELOPING COUNTRIES FACING NEW DETERMINANTS AND CUSTOMS ROLES

Czysowich[180] cites typical problems developing countries face to apply determinants of Future Customs Policy and to fulfill customs missions. They are: cumbersome procedures, lack of uniformity, little co-operation between customs administrations, inadequate, ineffective or non-existent computerisation, mandatory 100%controls which are complicated and costly, tracking

[180] *Op.cit.*, 2008, p.28.

the goods, valuation, little integration with the private sector and insufficient security.

However, our experience reveals that a part from typical problems mentioned above, there are some additional difficulties which hamper the implementation of determinants and customs missions in developing countries. They are hereafter.

C. DIFFICUTIES FOR DEVELOPING COUNTRIES TO APPLY DETERMINANTS AND CUSTOMS MISSIONS

Our professional experience as an intelligence analyst, technical attaché to the RILO-CA and customs officer

Considering for example the recommendation of the Customs Co-operation Council on the operation of the Global network of Regional Intelligence Liaison Offices (RILOS), the Article (2) recommends that in order to protect society, secure revenue and effectively combat customs offences, Members should establish RILOS covering all WCO regions[181].

To put that in other words, RILOS are very important to help customs administrations fulfill their missions on the ground. So, are customs administrations for RILOS. However, our experience from the RILO-CA seems to be bitter in that in spite of commitment taken by their administration affiliated Members, some Officers do not understand the role of RILOS. That is why, they do not cooperate at all with them. Information got here and there reveals that this lack of sufficient cooperation and other

[181] World Customs Organisation, Recommendations of the Customs Co-operation Council on the operation of the Global network of Regional Intelligence Liaison Office (RILOS).

difficulties occur even among Officers inside different customs administrations and may probably be additional ones developing countries face while applying determinants and fulfilling customs missions on the ground. Without going deeply into the matter these difficulties are: fraud, corruption, discrimination, cooperation, motivation, integrity (…). The list is not exhaustive. The WCO sustains, "Customs Administrations of the WCA Region are facing the huge challenge of considerable political interference in personnel management, both from the view-points of staff recruitment and mobility"[182].

After identifying developing countries difficulties to apply determinants and customs missions, let us see the situation in the DRC customs.

D. THE SPECIFIC CASE OF THE DRC

1. Difficulties for the DRC customs administration to implement new determinants and missions

In fact, after the implementation of customs reform and modernization and due to its authorities' management, the Congolese customs is considered as one of the best national services in recent years.

However, inspite of this achievement, as a developing country, some of the difficulties mentioned in the previous item exist in the DRC customs as well. It is the case with front line officers while performing their job on the ground. These difficulties are challenges for its customs administration to face new determinants and apply its missions perfectly. In the DRC, they are commonly called in French, 'ANTI-VALEURS' in English, "anti-values".

[182] World Customs Organization Study on the challenges of the West and Central Africa Region of world customs Organisation, p. 7.

They are: integrity, fraud, little cooperation among front line officers and other agencies (…). A part from that, mention can be made also of: valuation, goods classification, capacity buildings, elaboration of external statistics (…).

2. Remedies by the DRC ruling committee to face anti-values

To challenge anti-values and other issues mentioned above, the DRC customs has reformed its structural framework and made a lot of actions. Concerning structures, mention can be made of: creation of directorates of Tariff and Rules of Origin to deal with issues relating to goods origin and classification, Brigade and Enforcement to fight against smuggling or any kind of fraud including matters relating to intelligence, Statistics and Economic studies to elaborate external statistics, Human Resources including training for staff capacity building issues, etc.

Talking about other actions there are: controls in departure or export, cooperation with: neighbouring countries by signing Mutual Administrative Assistances (MAA), regional and international organisations police and private sector by signining Memorandum of Understanding (MOU), application of the Arusha declaration (promoting ethics is a must obligation at the DRC customs) and the Framework of Standards.

The DRC customs has signed a lot of MAA with different administrations such: Belgium, Central African Republic, Congo, South Africa, Tanzania, Kenya, (…) and MOU with Vlisco.

Furthermore, as a WCO member the DRC customs applies the WCO tools and instruments namely the use of CEN and its applications; CEN, CENcomm and nCEN (on going), IPM, participates in the WCO activities and those organized by the WCO different partners such as; Interpol, UNODC (…). The list is not exhaustive. See also social actions...

3. Remedies suggested by the present work to face new determinants and apply customs missions

This book sustains the policy implemented by the DGDA and suggests that the DRC customs should continue to strengthen the same policy while facing all issues mentioned in the previous item. It must put emphasis on the training of officers to the use of CEN and its applications in case of intelligence issues, implement the IPR section, use of IPM and INFO_IPR to combat counterfeiting and piracy and protect Intellectual Property Rights, cooperation with air companies, seaway companies, use of delivery control techniques, ratifying the Medicrime convention (this concerns the Ministry of Health and customs may create an incentive on this issue)…continue to sign memorandum of Understaning and Mutual Assistance (…).

4. Post-period of customs reform and modernisation

An interesting question we can ask is, what will happen after the implementation of the 2003 customs reform and modernisation programme?

Accordingly, this question arises another future for the DRC customs which is to follow up, evaluate and update the Reform and modernization programme. Thanks to the DRC customs experts on this issue since another programme has been elaborated since 2010.

For readers' information, the reform to be implemented within the framework of this 2010 programme comprises the following axes: strategic management, the service oriented culture(relationship with the user), the legal framework, the organisational structure, resource management, procedures and controls, the fight against fraud, the excise products control device, the foreign trade statistics, new information and communication technologies[183]. Since the 2010 programme is devoted to 2013-2015, this book does not make of it its concern.

[183] Direction Générale des Douanes et Accises (DGDA), Le nouveau Programme de Réforme et Modernisation douanière.

CONCLUSION

As the World Customs Organization Enforcement Committee (EC) recognised during its 36th session, international customs community faces new challenges. As important stakeholders within this community, customs administrations have to identify these challenges and combat them. Eg. fighting against illicit trade of elephants in the Congo basin in Central Africa.

This relates to our book in that we have identified an issue which arose in 2003. That is, the implementation of customs reform and modernisation programme which brought a revolution at the DRC customs management. We presented the programme facts or keys, we went through them and proposed some solutions in case the DRC wants to elaborate any customs reform and modernisation programme in the future.

After being through this work, the conclusion we can draw is that as far as customs policy is concerned, the 2003 programme of customs reform and modernisation appears to be the customs policy of the DRC from 2003 to 2010. So, it is worth reminding that the modernisation of customs administration requires fundamental changes in both the environment within which the customs administration works and the way in which it undertakes its activities.

As said in chapter 4, Change is required in four key areas: establishing coherent trade policies and clear supporting legislation, adopting modern, simple procedures, shifting to substantial reliance on self-assessment by tax-payers, supported by movement from physical to post-release controls and ensuring incentive and organisational structures conducive to integrity and effectiveness in customs administration.

This work suggests that any change which will occur in customs reform and modernisation in the DRC continues to fall within this framework. It also suggests that an evaluation of each elaborated programme should be made after a certain period to reintegrate and add acceptable comments in order to produce another new programme of reform and modernisation.

BIBLIOGRAPHY

A- PUBLISHED WORKS

ASAKURA H. (2003). *World history of the customs and tariffs*. Brussels, World Customs Organization.

BABA KAKÉ Ibrahima. (1985). *Combats pour l'histoire africaine*. Paris, Présence africaine.

BABUDAA MALIBATO. (1990). *Condensé du cours complet*, 6è secondaire, Nathan, Paris.

DEWULF, SOKOL josé B. (2005). *Customs modernization, Handbook.* World Bank.

Direction Générale des Douanes et Accises de la RDC. (2010-2013). *Le nouveau Programme de Réforme et Modernisation douanière.*

Ecole des douanes de Neuilly sur seine. (2002-2003). *Présentation de l'espèce tarifaire.*

ESAMBA Bokel'Ipoka. (2008). *Counterfeiting and Piracy in import and export; A strategy of the DRCongo* (MA Thesis). University of Munster, Germany.

KAYEMBE Aaron Cianyi. (2015). *Deo Rugwiza, une décennie d'un management basé sur la bonne gouvernance et l'éthique professionnelle*. Kinshasa.

KEEN Michael. (2003). *Changing customs; Challenges and Strategies for the Reform of Customs Administration.* International Monetary Fund.

KIZERBO Joseph. (1978). *Histoire de l'Afrique noire d'hier à demain*. Paris, Hatier.

LUX Michael. (2002). *Guide to Community Customs Legislation*. Bruxelles, Bruylant.

MOKHTAR G. (1981). *Histoire Générale de l'Afrique*, II : l'Afrique ancienne. Paris, Présence africaine, Edicef, Unesco.

MWANGE Muteba. (2006). *L'Analyse de l'incidence du Guichet Unique sur les recettes de l'Etat au Port de Matadi*. Kinshasa, Université Pédagogique Nationale.

Office des Douanes et Accises. (2003). *Programme de réforme et modernisation douanière.*

Office des Douanes et Accises. (2003). *Tarif des Droits et Taxes à l'importation et à l'exportation.* Kinshasa-Limete, Shekinah.

Présidence de la République Démocratique du Congo. (2010). Loi N°10/002 du 20 août 2010 portant Code des Douanes.

TENDAY Alain. (2014). *Les procédures douanières en RDC ; expérience du « guichet unique » au poste de Matadi*. Paris, L'Harmattan.

United Nations Conference on Trade and Development. (1997). *Handbook of world Mineral Trade Statistics 1991-1996.*United Nations, New York and Geneva.

United Nations Educational, Scientific and Cultural Organization. (1970). Convention on the means of prohibiting and preventing the illicit import, export and transfer of ownership of cultural property. Paris.

United Nations. (2006). *Trade Facilitation Handbook, Part II: Technical Notes on Essential, Trade Facilitation Measures*. United Nations, New York and Geneva.

WEHMEIER Sally. (2000). *Oxford advanced Learner's Dictionary*. Oxford University Press.

World Customs Organization. (1977)

International Convention on Mutual Administrative Assistance for the prevention, investigation and repression of offences, Nairobi Convention.

World Customs Organization. (1979). Arusha Declaration.

World Customs Organization. (2000). Revised Kyoto Convention. Brussels.

World Customs Organization. (2015). Punta Cana Resolution, Resolution of the Policy Commission of the World Customs Organization on the role of Customs in the security context.

World Customs Organization. Convention on Harmonised System.

World Customs Organization. (2018). Diary.

World Customs Organization. Recommendations of the Customs Co-operation Council on the operation of the Global network of Regional Intelligence Liaison Offices (RILOS).

World Customs Organization. Strategic Trade Control Enforcement (STCE) implementation Guide.

World Health Organization. (2013). Protocol to eliminate illicit trade in Tobacco products. Geneva.

World Trade Organization. (1999). *The Legal Texts, the Results of the Uruguay Round of Multilateral Trade Negotiations*. Cambridge University Press.

World Trade Organization. (2010). *Trade Policy Review.* Democratic Republic of the Congo.

World Trade Organization. (2016). *Trade Policy Review.* Democratic Republic of the Congo.

B- JOURNALS OR NEWSPAPERS, MAGAZINES, RADIO PRESS, UNPUBLISHED WORKS, WEB SITES AND OTHERS

I. JOURNALS, NEWSPAPERS OR MAGAZINES

1. Administration des douanes congolaises. (2010). « La Modernisation en marche ». *Revue des Douanes Congolaises*, n°006, Boulevard du 30 juin, Kinshasa-Gombe.

2. Administration des douanes congolaises. (2013). « La Modernisation en marche ». *Revue des Douanes Congolaises*, n°009, Boulevard du 30 juin, Kinshasa-Gombe.

3. Administration des douanes congolaises. (2015). « 2005-2015 :10ans de reformes et performances ». *Revue des Douanes Congolaises*, Numéro spécial, septembre, Boulevard du 30 juin, Kinshasa-Gombe.

II. RADIO PRESS

B-One Radio TV, Democratic Republic of Congo.

III. UNPUBLISHED WORKS AND NOTES OF COURSES

CZYZOWICZ Wieslaw. (2007). Customs Policy Module-Challenges and future (Master of Customs Administration Course). University of Muenster.

CZYZOWICZ Wieslaw. (2008). Customs Policy Module-Legal and Practical Approach.

CZYZOWICZ Wieslaw. (2008). Customs Policy Module-Theoretical approach. University of Muenster.

Feng X. (2006). Regional Trade policy Course, Introduction to the WTO Legal Affairs Office, WTO Secretariat. Windhoek.

HARRISON Mark. (2008). Customs Management Theory and Practice. Lectures notes prepared for the University of Munster.

KRALOVA Eva. (2008). *Tariff and Trade Affairs Directorate* (Master of Customs Administration Programme). Muenster University.

LEWIS Gareth. (2008). World Customs Data Model; about Single Window. Muenster University.

MIHIGO Uguha. (2006-2007). Rapport de stage effectué à l'Office des Douanes et Accises. Kinshasa, Gombe.

ROGMANN Achim. (2008). *Customs valuation Law: the EU Model.*

ROGMANN Achim. (2008). *Principles of WTO (*Master of Customs Administration), University of Muenster.

ROGMANN Achim. (2008). *The Multilateral Trade System of the WTO: Basic Principles*, Fachhochschule Braunschweig/Wolfenbüttel. University of Applied Sciences, Brunswick European Law School.

SIMBABO Jean-pierre. (2000-2001). Rapport de stage effectué à la Direction Générale de l'Ofida. Kinshasa, Gombe.

World Customs Organization. (2004). *Annual report.*

World Customs Organization. (2008). Data model, About Single Window, Data Model training. Munster.

World Customs Organization. *35th Enforcement Committee Executive Report.*

IV. PAPERS

MUBIBYA Silutala. (2015). L'incidence du démembrement des provinces de la République Démocratique du Congo sur les activités douanières. 10ème session des Directeurs Centraux et Provinciaux.

World Customs Organization. Security Project for West and Central Africa (customs counter-terrorism initiative for West and Central Africa).

World Customs Organization. Programme Global Shield.

V.WEB SITES

1. https:Afr.wikipedia.org/wiki/royaume-kuba
2. htpps: //en.wikipedia.org/wiki/berlin-conference
3. www.infoplease.com/country/democratic-Republic-of-congo.html
4. http://www.questiaschool.com /read/1G1-224534703/the-curse
5. www.indexmundicom/democratie_republic of congo/natural_ressources.html
6. www.questiaschool.com/read/191-224534703/the-curse
7. http://en.wikipedia.org/wiki/democratic_republic_of_the_congo
8. www.douane.gouv.fr
9. www.musse-douanes.fr/documentation/25-histoire-de-la-douane.html.fr
10. https://en.wikipedia.org/wiki/cotonou_Agreement
11. https://en.wikipedia.org/wiki/Excise
12. Collins.inhttp://dictionary.reverso.net/English

13. https://www.the positiveencouraging.global/carl-rogers-and-the-person-ce
14. https://en.wikipedia.org/wiki/small-Arms_and_lihgt_weapons
15. https://www.belastingdienst.nl/wps/wcm/connectbldcontenten/belastingdienst/customs/safetyhealth-economy and environment/cdiu cluster/strategic goods/strategic goods
16. http://lawin.org/Brussels- definition of value
17. www.google.com
18. www.thebalance.com/what-is-the-doha-round-of-trade-talks-3306365.
19. https://www.wikipedia.org/wiki/Bali_package
20. http://en.wikipedia.org/wiki/economic_community_of_the_great_lake_country
21. www.sadc.int
22. https://en.wikipedia.org/wiki/common_market_for_Eastern_and_Southern_Africa
23. https://en.wikipedia.org/wiki/Economic_community_of_central_African_state
24. www.wcoomd.org
25. https://en.wikipedia.org/wiki/world_trade_organization
26. http://www.un.org/en/sections/history/history-united-nations/
27. htpps://whatis.techtarget.com/definition/certification
28. https://www.businessdictionnary.com/definition/certification.html
29. www.igi-global.com

TABLE OF CONTENTS

FOREWORD 5

DEDICATION 7

ACKNOWLEDGMENTS 9

ABBREVIATIONS 13

OUTLINE 19

INTRODUCTION 21

CHAPTER 1 AN OVERVIEW OF THE DEMOCRATIC REPUBLIC OF CONGO AND ITS CUSTOMS ADMINISTRATION 25

- A. BRIEF ACCOUNT OF THE DEMOCRATIC REPUBLIC OF CONGO 25
  - I. Historical aspect 25
    - 1. Pre-Colonial Period 25
    - 2. Colonial Period 27
    - 3. Post Independence Period 27
  - II. Geographic aspect 29
  - III. Economic aspect 29
  - IV. Cultural aspect 30
  - V. Linguistic aspect 31
- B. DEMOCRATIC REPUBLIC OF CONGO CUSTOMS ADMINISTRATION 32
  - I. A short glance at the history of customs and its missions 32
  - II. The DRC customs before independence 34

III. The DRC customs after independence (from the 15th 1979 to date) 35
CHAPTER 2 THE BASICS OF CUSTOMS POLICY .. 39
A. PROBLEMATIC DEFINITION OF CUSTOMS POLICY 39
B. OBJECTS OF CUSTOMS POLICY 42
C. ELEMENTS OF CUSTOMS POLICY 42
D. SOURCES OF CUSTOMS POLICY 43
I. Economic sources 43
II. National legal sources 48
III. International legal sources 48
E. FUNCTIONS OF CUSTOMS POLICY 49
I. Promotional function 49
II. Protective function 50
III. Preferential function 50
IV. Fiscal function 51
V. Retorsion function 52
VI. Adaptation international norms and standards .. 52
F. INSTRUMENTS OF CUSTOMS POLICY 52
I. Customs laws 52
II. Customs administration 56
G. CUSTOMS POLICY CREATORS 59
I. National level 59
II. International level 61
H. MEASURES OF CUSTOMS POLICY 62
I. Tariff policy 62
II. Non-tariffs policy 64
CHAPTER 3 THE SECURITY MISSION OF CUSTOMS 65

A. THE IMPORTANCE OF THE SECURITY MISSION OF CUSTOMS....66
B. SECURITY MISSION LEGAL BASIS....67
I. The Revised Kyoto Convention....67
II. The UN 1540 Resolution....67
III. The Punta Cana Resolution....69
IV. Counter-terrorism strategy....69
C. THE WCO SECURITY PROGRAMME....69
D. OUR VIEW POINT RELATING TO THE CONTRIBUTION OF RESOLUTIONS 1540 AND PUNTA CANA TO THE SECURITY MISSION OF CUSTOMS....73
E. LESSONS AND SUGGESTIONS TO THE DRC CUSTOMS RELATING TO STCE....77
CHAPTER 4 THE CUSTOMS POLICY OF THE DEMOCRATIC REPUBLIC OF CONGO FROM 2003 TO 2010....79
A. CUSTOMS REFORM AND MODERNISATION PROGRAMME....79
B. CUSTOMS REFORM AND MODERNISATION IN THE DEMOCRATIC REPUBLIC OF CONGO....82
I. Simplification and facilitation of customs procedures....83
II. Optimisation of the mechanism of combating fraud....84
III. Reorganisation of services....84
IV. The 2003 programme measures....85
V. Some key issues of reform and modernisation in the DRC....86
1. Legislation....86
a) Customs legislation....86
b) Excise legislation....87

c) Connected legislations 89
2. Single window or customs automation 89
3. Tariff measures 90
a) Tariff 90
b) Non tariff measures 93
4. Valuation 94
a) Brussels definition of valuation 94
b) Valuation according to General Agreement on Tariffs and Trade (GATT): article VII 95
5. Customs revue 104
6. Capacity building 104
C. COOPERATION WITH REGIONAL AND INTERNATIONAL ORGANISATIONS 105
I. Regional level 107
1. The DRC customs and ECGLC (CEPGL) 107
2. The DRC customs and SADC 107
3. The DRC customs and COMESA 109
4. The DRC customs and Economic Community of Central African States (ECCAS) 111
II. International level 112
1. DRC customs and the World Customs Organisation 112
2. DRC customs and World Trade Organisation (WTO) 122
3. DRC Customs and United Nations 124
CHAPTER 5 THE FUTURE OF CUSTOMS POLICY OF THE DRC 127
A. DETERMINANTS OF FUTURE CUSTOMS POLICY 127
I. Integration of the non-revenue tasks in security context 127
II. From physical checks at one point towards certification of the whole supply chain 128

III. From executor to coordinator of the data and checks on goods having a third country as place of origin or destination executor 129
IV. Digital era 129
V. Additional determinants 131
B. DEVELOPING COUNTRIES FACING NEW DETERMINANTS AND CUSTOMS ROLES 133
C. DIFFICUTIES FOR DEVELOPING COUNTRIES TO APPLY DETERMINANTS AND CUSTOMS MISSIONS 134
D. THE SPECIFIC CASE OF THE DRC 135
1. Difficulties for the DRC customs administration to implement new determinants and missions 135
2. Remedies by the DRC ruling committee to face anti-values 136
3. Remedies suggested by the present work to face new determinants and apply customs missions 137
4. Post-period of customs reform and modernisation 137
CONCLUSION 139
BIBLIOGRAPHY 141

Structures éditoriales du groupe L'Harmattan

L'Harmattan Italie
Via degli Artisti, 15
10124 Torino
harmattan.italia@gmail.com

L'Harmattan Hongrie
Kossuth l. u. 14-16.
1053 Budapest
harmattan@harmattan.hu

L'Harmattan Sénégal
10 VDN en face Mermoz
BP 45034 Dakar-Fann
senharmattan@gmail.com

L'Harmattan Cameroun
TSINGA/FECAFOOT
BP 11486 Yaoundé
inkoukam@gmail.com

L'Harmattan Burkina Faso
Achille Somé – tengnule@hotmail.fr

L'Harmattan Guinée
Almamya, rue KA 028 OKB Agency
BP 3470 Conakry
harmattanguinee@yahoo.fr

L'Harmattan RDC
185, avenue Nyangwe
Commune de Lingwala – Kinshasa
matangilamusadila@yahoo.fr

L'Harmattan Congo
67, boulevard Denis-Sassou-N'Guesso
BP 2874 Brazzaville
harmattan.congo@yahoo.fr

L'Harmattan Mali
Sirakoro-Meguetana V31
Bamako
syllaka@yahoo.fr

L'Harmattan Togo
Djidjole – Lomé
Maison Amela
face EPP BATOME
ddamela@aol.com

L'Harmattan Côte d'Ivoire
Résidence Karl – Cité des Arts
Abidjan-Cocody
03 BP 1588 Abidjan
espace_harmattan.ci@hotmail.fr

L'Harmattan Algérie
22, rue Moulay-Mohamed
31000 Oran
info2@harmattan-algerie.com

L'Harmattan Maroc
5, rue Ferrane-Kouicha, Talaâ-Elkbira
Chrableyine, Fès-Médine
30000 Fès
harmattan.maroc@gmail.com

Nos librairies en France

Librairie internationale
16, rue des Écoles – 75005 Paris
librairie.internationale@harmattan.fr
01 40 46 79 11
www.librairieharmattan.com

Lib. sciences humaines & histoire
21, rue des Écoles – 75005 Paris
librairie.sh@harmattan.fr
01 46 34 13 71
www.librairieharmattansh.com

Librairie l'Espace Harmattan
21 bis, rue des Écoles – 75005 Paris
librairie.espace@harmattan.fr
01 43 29 49 42

Lib. Méditerranée & Moyen-Orient
7, rue des Carmes – 75005 Paris
librairie.mediterranee@harmattan.fr
01 43 29 71 15

Librairie Le Lucernaire
53, rue Notre-Dame-des-Champs – 75006 Paris
librairie@lucernaire.fr
01 42 22 67 13

www.ingramcontent.com/pod-product-compliance
Lightning Source LLC
Chambersburg PA
CBHW071345230926
51846CB00002B/456
* 9 7 8 2 3 4 3 1 7 7 1 0 6 *